RIGHT TO

A CELEBRATION OF
THE SHEFFIELD CAMPAIGN FOR ACCESS
TO MOORLAND

Give me a great big hill and a rolling sky
And a pair of legs to guide me by,
A map and a compass if you will,
But pray first give me that big hill.

G.H.B. Ward, 1932

Compiled by
DAVE SISSONS

Edited by
ROLY SMITH

ISBN 0-901100-60-9

Published jointly by
Northend Creative Print Solutions
Clyde Road, Sheffield S8 0TZ
and
SCAM, 334 Manchester Road, Sheffield S10 5DQ

Title Page: New Cross Road, Bradfield. 2001. (Terry Howard)

Designed and Printed by NORTHEND CREATIVE PRINT SOLUTIONS

CONTENTS

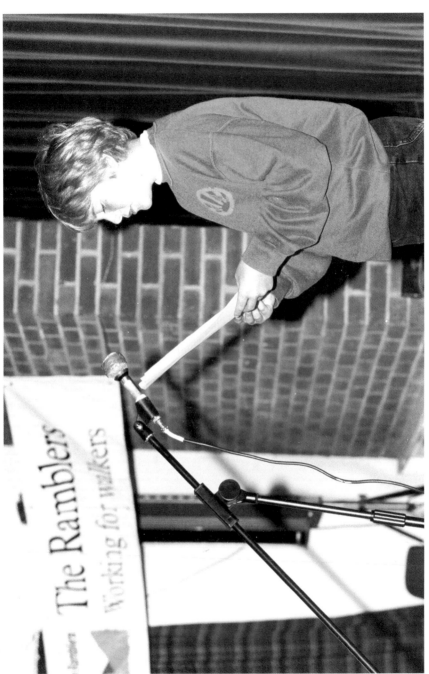

Looking to the Future: Richard Howard, son of SCAM Secretary Terry Howard, became the youngest-ever speaker at an access rally when he addressed a meeting at Hope Valley College on his 13th birthday in 1997. (Ramblers' Association)

FOREWORD – A Worthy SCAM

by Mike Harding

I am lucky enough to have known two of the finest men in the outdoor movement: Benny Rothman and Tom Stephenson, members of that old school of Socialist walkers, idealists and activists - when Socialism and Idealism were not dirty words. And though they worked in different ways - Benny, vocal and confrontational; Tom, quieter, politically-astute and just as determined - they had a common aim: the right of the people of these islands to roam at will on land which had once been open to everyone.

But though Tom and Benny might have been among the most visible of those working for the freedom of the moors and mountains, they were part of a greater movement of thousands of men and women working in organisations like the Ramblers' Association, Red Rope and SCAM, or beavering away quietly as individuals. The pressure of this common effort over many years has finally and literally moved mountains, and we are now in a position where our mountains and moors are being opened up to us once again.

But we're not out of the woods yet and, as the land is being mapped for access, there are threats to its beauty and its wildness: wind farms, off-road vehicles, quarrying extensions and other threats are hanging on there in the wings for the next generation of idealists and visionaries to do battle with. Yet there is time for us at least to pause and applaud the work of all those who, like SCAM, battled, for no profit and little recognition, to get us thus far. When you look at the power and vested interests ranged against them, you can see that it was no mean feat.

As the Irish singer-songwriter John Spillane once wrote in one of his songs:

Well done everybody, well done.
Were we brilliant or what?

Mike Harding compères the 70th anniversary celebration of the Kinder Mass Trespass in 2002. (Dave Sissons)

5

INTRODUCTION

by Dave Sissons

The Countryside and Rights of Way (CROW) Act, 2000 was a major landmark in the prolonged battle for public access to uncultivated land in the UK, and it marked the successful culmination of more than a century of on-and-off campaigning. It is arguable that the CROW Act would not have emerged from Parliament, certainly not as early as 2000, without sustained pressure on key individuals and organisations over nearly two decades by the Sheffield-based organisation, Sheffield Campaign for Access to Moorland (SCAM).

More than any other organisation, SCAM led the way through the 1980s and 1990s with its policy of direct action, reviving the same tactic of mass trespass which had been used by access campaigners before the Second World War, the most legendary occasion being the 1932 Kinder Scout Mass Trespass. SCAM acted as a ginger group on the Ramblers' Association, which in turn lobbied the Labour Party, especially during the latter decade or so of its 18 years in opposition (1979-97), urging it to include in its party manifesto a commitment to the passing through Parliament of a new Right to Roam Act.

On Sunday, September 19, 2004, SCAM's aims seemed more or less achieved, but the organisation has not disbanded, its members and supporters being determined not to forget the lessons of the past. When the 1949 National Parks and Access to the Countryside Act was passed by the Attlee Labour Government, a previous generation of access campaigners, growing up in the 1920s and 1930s, seemed to think it had achieved its aims and could rest on its laurels. As Marion Shoard described it, 'The passions which had provoked the Kinder Scout mêlée seemed to belong to a bygone age, as people concerned themselves with acquiring new council homes, consumer durables to put inside them, and cars to park in the driveway. Freedom to wander the great outdoors was of little concern to a nation intent on pursuing domestic prosperity' (*A Right to Roam*, Oxford University Press, 1999).

Some of those same access campaigners, later disillusioned with the slow progress made under the 1949 Act, were, in the early 1980s, to meet a younger generation of access campaigners which had grown up in the 1950s and 1960s and had started to direct some of its radical optimism, bred of the anti-Vietnam War campaign of the late 1960s, to environmental concerns closer to home. It was from such a meeting of generations that SCAM emerged in Sheffield in 1982.

Opposite: The historic photograph of the 1932 Mass Trespass – walkers move off alongside the Kinder river. (Peak District National Park)

THE ORIGINS OF SCAM

by Dave Sissons

In 1981 the UK's first National Park, the Peak District, celebrated its 30th anniversary. In the Sheffield *Morning Telegraph* of October 12, 1981, another anniversary was heralded in an article by Tim Brown - the 50th anniversary of the Kinder Scout Mass Trespass of Sunday April 24, 1932. The article stated that, 'Organising committees based in Hayfield and Manchester hope to bring together many of the trespassers of 1932 for a full day of organised walks and other special events', and 'Mr John Beadle, chairman of the Peak Park Planning Board, will unveil a commemorative plaque in the disused quarry where ramblers from Manchester mustered before their historic confrontation with a private army of gamekeepers on the grouse moor high above the village.'

The article went on to say, 'The long fight for a legal right of access to mountains ended in a qualified victory under the 1945 Labour Government'. This provoked a response from Roy Bullen, then working for Derbyshire County Council as Area Careers Officer for the High Peak and Derbyshire Dales, and a long-standing member of the Ramblers' Association.

The Kinder Scout 50th Anniversary Celebration, Kinder Road, April 1982. (Terry Howard)

In the *Morning Telegraph* of October 21, 1981, Roy Bullen wrote, '*Qualified* is the correct description, for there are still many areas of wild country to which the public do not have the same legal rights as they now enjoy on Kinder. As Howard Hill showed in his book *Freedom to Roam* (parts of which were serialised in the *Morning Telegraph*), there are still some 27 moors in the Peak and southern Pennines alone for which access agreements (or access orders) have yet to be made. Many country-goers believe the protracted negotiations between National Park authorities and moor owners are being delayed unnecessarily. While fully acknowledging the very important access agreements negotiated by the Peak Park Board in its earlier years, the public must not imagine the ramblers' campaign is over. The gathering near Hayfield next April must, besides celebrating what has been achieved, focus sharply upon what the Peak Park Board and other National Park authorities still have to accomplish.'

Roy Bullen was later to write, in a leaflet on *The Early Days of the Sheffield Campaign for Access to Moorland* (SCAM), distributed to SCAM members: 'Quite some time after this Letter to the Editor was published, a young man called to invite me to join an organisation being formed to gain access to all local moorlands. He said my letter had helped get the pressure group started'. This was probably in the spring of 1982 - Roy remembers it was still daylight when he had this visit in the early evening after he'd got home from work - and there may have been two young men, rather than just one. Jon Cowley and his friend Dick Williams had heard of the plans being made in Hayfield and Manchester to celebrate the 1932 Kinder Scout Mass Trespass, and both were keen to get something similar going in Sheffield.

The notice of the inaugural meeting in 1982.

Both Jon Cowley and Dick Williams had Socialist Workers' Party (SWP) connections, John having joined the International Socialists (later called the SWP) around 1968 and Dick having joined the SWP in 1980. However the SWP itself had no connection with the initiation of the organisation that became SCAM. Jon and Dick were members of the socialist walkers' and climbers' club, Red Rope, and it was probably from the Red Rope grapevine that they heard about the plans for the Kinder Scout Mass Trespass 50th Anniversary celebrations. Nevertheless the SWP would have given them good organisational and agitational skills, and it would be these skills that were applied to the setting up of a Sheffield committee to work in tandem with the Hayfield and Manchester committees.

In January 1982, fliers were distributed around Sheffield advertising an 'Open Planning Meeting' at the Bow Centre in Holly Street on Monday, February 8. Organisers, Jon and Dick, were pleasantly surprised to see that the meeting was well-attended, with about 30 people turning up. These included a contingent of older ramblers like John and Irene Bunting, Archie Brearley, Walter Grocock, Bill Keen, George Fowler and Jack Burling, who soon impressed on the meeting that the struggle for access, which had burst into national media publicity in 1932, was far from over. There was access to Kinder and Bleaklow but there was still a vast area of private moorland to the west of Sheffield where no access agreements existed.

So, in addition to rallying support for the planned celebrations in Hayfield in April, the meeting decided to organise an event similar to the 1932 Kinder trespass on some of this non-access moorland to the immediate west of Sheffield. Bamford Moor was selected and Sunday, March 28 was chosen as the date.

A Sheffield Organising Committee led by Dick and Jon was formed and met regularly in the run up to the Bamford Moor trespass and the Kinder celebration. Dick Williams writes: 'The memory fades a bit but I do have recollections of a very significant and early Bow Centre meeting involving Marion Shoard and Dave Cook. There was also a sequence of public meetings involving Jim Perrin, Jim Byford, Stephen Morton, the chair of the Peak Park Planning Board and many others. It was a very exciting time. The Bow meetings became very high profile and proposed the Organising Committee for the Kinder Celebrations from which SCAM later in 1982 evolved. Both Jon and I were the main impetus for this.'

Sunday, March 28 was the beginning of British Summer Time and a lot of people forgot to put their clocks forward, missing relevant transport connections. Despite this little hiccup, the Bamford Moor mass trespass turned out to be a tremendous success, far exceeding expectations. Around 300 people turned up, with journalists and camera crews present at least at the start, most of them being not exactly dressed for the occasion. Though deprived of a skirmish, the press and television journalists gave good coverage, and it encouraged the committee to plan a programme of further mass trespasses.

The Kinder Scout 50th Anniversary Celebration at Bowden Bridge Quarry, Hayfield, April 1982. (SCAM)

The main Kinder Scout 50th Anniversary Celebrations duly took place on April 24 in Hayfield, with a few Manchester and Hayfield organisers being a bit miffed at the Sheffield organisers stealing a march on them with the Bamford Moor event. There was much media attention plus the presence of the rambling and outdoors 'establishment'.

The Sheffield group followed the successes of Bamford Moor and the Kinder 50th with another public meeting on Monday, May 17 to plan future strategy. At this meeting it was decided that the 'Sheffield Organising Committee' sounded a bit old hat and non-descript, even though it produced a punchy acronym. A catchier name for the emerging organisation was sought and the meeting settled for Sheffield Campaign for Access to Moorland, which produced the memorable acronym SCAM - memorable especially a few years later when the American slang term meaning 'a swindle or con-trick' gained currency in the UK. A further mass trespass was planned for Sunday, June 27, and the target this time was Bradfield Moors, owned by Fitzwilliam Estates.

11

THE GENTLE ART OF TRESPASSING

There was a time, long ago, when I would suggest a route to the Wanderer before we set out; but I have come to realise that his own plan is the better - to climb, or open, the first gate that chances to be near, and to go forward, choosing constantly to trespass whenever possible. This business of trespassing is little understood, and deserves a random treatise devoted solely to a description of its joys, its griefs, its difficulties. To the uninitiated, trespass is a fearsome matter, involving - in the event of detection - prosecution, an appearance before the ogres of the law, and afterwards a long vista, beginning with fines and penalties, and ending with the modern equivalent of Botany Bay. To experts, though, it is a simple game and a delightful one.

Like all games, it has its strict rules and also its more delicately shaded laws of etiquette. The Complete Trespasser, for instance, must never leave a gate open which he found closed; must not take a bee-line across growing wheat or through ripening meadow grass; must repair a dry-built wall if he chances to bring it down with him - no rare happening in a limestone country - while climbing it. The righteous trespasser, moreover, should on no occasion be discovered uprooting lilies of the valley, oak fern, or wild orchids, nor should he move forward with a high head when summoned to stand his ground. When crossing a moor at breeding time, it is not strictly courteous - according to trespasser's etiquette - to put one's boot into the nests of breeding grouse; nor should one, in passing through a wood, throw one's stick at pheasants rising close at hand. It is well, too, if you see a big trout idling in a shady pool, to avoid the temptation to lie down - a boy again - and gently tickle him until you land him on the bank.

These would seem obvious axioms; but I have seen such total ignorance of them displayed so frequently that it may be well to set them down. The niceties of the game - those impalpable lights and shades which only the practised hand can grasp - I cannot enter into here, for the Wanderer and I are busy climbing hills and scrambling down the further steeps.

From *A Benedict in Arcady* - Halliwell Sutcliffe (quoted in the *Sheffield Clarion Ramblers' Handbook*, 1914-15).

Rallying for the Bamford Moor mass trespass on March 28, 1982, at the car park by the A57.
(Terry Howard)

The notice of an early SCAM trespass on Big Moor.

SCAM

TRESPASSERS P.W.I.L.L. BE.

BIG MOOR
Mass Trespass
Sunday May 15th at 11am

Recently the Water Board agreed to sell Big Moor (which includes Froggat Edge) to the Peak Park Planning Board. The government has since intervened to order the Water Board to sell to the highest bidder which is likely to be a farm...

This will inevitably mean c...

limited rights of...

MEMORIES

An Unlikely Ally

by Howard Hill

Howard Hill was born in Sheffield and began work in the 1920s as an underground apprentice electrician in the Yorkshire coalfield. After a spell of unemployment during the 1930s, he found work in a Sheffield steelworks and was also at one time a trade union organiser for deep-sea fishermen in trawlers sailing out of Hull. During this period he was a regular rambler on the Peak District hills and moors, and he was present on the Kinder Scout and Abbey Brook mass trespasses of 1932. Before his death in 1980 he was Secretary of the Access Committee of the South Yorkshire and North East Derbyshire Ramblers' Association (SYNED RA).

With Tom Stephenson, Howard had attended a conference organised by the Peak National Park at Losehill Hall on February 23-24, 1979, the subject being moorland management and access. There were 65 people in attendance, including six moor owners, one of whom was the Duke of Devonshire. The Duke made what Howard and Tom regarded as the most remarkable speech of the whole weekend. Reporting back to SYNED RA, Howard wrote:

Left to right - the late Duke of Devonshire, Jack Burling and the late Bill Keen at the Kinder Mass Trespass 70th Anniversary Celebration in Hayfield, 2002. (Dave Sissons)

Three of the greatest access campaigners at the Cave Dale National Parks Rally in 1986. Left to right - Benny Rothman, Tom Stephenson, Stephen Morton. (Peak District National Park)

Neither of us thought we should ever listen to the type of speech he made, coming as he does from the other side of the social and political barrier. The Duke started out by declaring that he was now a walker; nay, even a rambler, and though he owned moorlands in Yorkshire on which grouse were shot, he himself was not a grouse shooter. He now walked the moorlands for pleasure, and amongst his walking achievements he numbered the Lyke Wake Walk.

Having turned his back on the grouse-shooting pastime of his forbears, his sympathies were now with the hikers. In fact he claimed that this particular aspect of class conflict - that between rambler and grouse shooter - had now disappeared. In consequence he was somewhat apprehensive as to how his grandfather and father, if alive, would view his conversion. He referred to the battle which took place between ramblers and his family over the attempts to gain legal access to Bolton Abbey Moors.

He put the blame for this at the door of the family's agent, claiming that the family knew the battle was lost before it even started, and consequently they should have conceded defeat with as much grace as they could muster, as this was the only way to foster better relations with the ramblers, who were in increasing numbers seeking the pleasures of upland walking. Nevertheless grouse shooting still continued on the Bolton Abbey Moors. After the first three weeks of the shooting season, when the estate is used by family and friends, it is let mainly to foreigners, from whom much-needed foreign currency is obtained.

He further justified grouse shooting, declaring that without it a lot of grouse would die of disease. He considered the two greatest dangers to the moors to be fires, which could be started carelessly, sometimes by glass, and dogs, which worried sheep. He further claimed that birds of prey and grouse do not go together, hence the need for good keepering.

G.H.B. Ward addresses the District Federation of Ramblers at a Winnats Pass Access Rally, 1933. (Ramblers' Association)

Tom welcomed the tenor of the Duke's speech and ended by inviting the Duke to join the Ramblers' Association. I echoed Tom's welcome and told how I had followed in the footsteps of Bert Ward and Edwin Royce, as a consequence of which I had often been chased by the earlier Duke's keepers, especially on the mass trespasses of 1932. If the Duke's present-day outlook was shared by his fellow moorland owners, why was only one third of the Peakland uplands covered by Access Agreements?

I pointed out that we ramblers shared his concern about the fire danger, as was shown by our unhesitating observance of access withdrawal during the drought of 1976, when the grouse shooters had still gone ahead with their shooting arrangements. I also pointed out that our members were foreign currency earners, working in factories throughout the year, producing goods for export, and we looked forward to the relaxing pleasures of walking the moorlands.

The Duke agreed that the behaviour of grouse shooters in 1976 had caused him some embarrassment at the time, and he came up after the speeches and shook hands with both of the Ramblers' Association representatives. I took the opportunity of mentioning my forthcoming book about the history of the access struggles, *Freedom to Roam*, which the Duke said he must get hold of and read. I couldn't help noticing that among the speakers, only Tom and I did not address the Duke as 'Your Grace'.

From the Winnats and Cave Dale

by John Bunting

There were many more younger people walking in the 1930s and 1940s, as working class lads did not have the opportunity to go to university. In those days we used our bikes to get us into the countryside and we left them at a tea room and then went for a walk.

I well remember the rallies in Winnats Pass. I went to my first rally in Winnats Pass in 1934 and was inspired by people like C.E.M. Joad, Bert Ward, Steve Morton and Phil Barnes, though to us kids they were like people from another planet. The Youth Hostels Association and the Cyclists Touring Club were very much involved in the early days - there were as many bikes as rucksacks on the grass.

After the War the rallies in Cave Dale were much more rambler-orientated as the Ramblers' Association organised them. We thought we had got what we wanted with the 1949 National Parks Act, but we were disappointed. During the War I trained as a gunner on the tank range on Midhope Moors. After the War it was the keepers who had the guns - they kept us off the moors when they could.

Things went a bit quiet for a while, until we formed SCAM. The 1932 Kinder Trespass was forgotten about for 30 years or so. One or two of us continued to trespass on a regular basis – Walter Grocock for instance led RA rambles on private moors, but with the permission of the land agents.

My wife Irene and I were founder members of SCAM and went on all the early trespasses. Roy Bullen first mentioned the idea of a ginger group, and Walter Grocock and I and one or two others thought it was time we did something to get things moving. SCAM's organised trespasses rekindled the access campaign. We later had great help and commitment from people like Kate Ashbrook and David Beskine of the Ramblers' Association, and we finally got the CROW Act in 2000.

The Ramblers' Association and SCAM

by Roy Bullen

Roy Bullen joined the Ramblers' Association in 1948 after returning from army service overseas, and he soon became Secretary of the rambling section of a Young People's Fellowship. At that time affiliated clubs like the YPF could attend RA Area Council meetings, and Roy was greatly influenced by veteran ramblers at these meetings, including Ted Spencer and G.H.B. Ward. Here he recalls his Ramblers' Association activity.

In the early 1950s some of us did voluntary warden (ranger) duties on Kinder on the access agreement land that had recently been obtained. From 1962 to 1968 I was part-time (weekends) Peak Park Information Centre Assistant at Edale and in the mobile caravan.

In the 1960s my career took me (via one and a half years in Doncaster) from Sheffield to north Lancashire, and we lived close to the Forest of Bowland, an Area of Outstanding Natural Beauty (AONB). Here a few of us started the Preston and Fylde Group of the Ramblers' Association (then part of the Lake District Area), which has now expanded into the Mid-Lancashire Area of the Association. Here I recruited Alan Howard, who was to become National Chairman of the Ramblers' Association – one of my more successful recruiting efforts! The Preston and Fylde Group began with two aims: to gain access to the forbidden moors of Bowland, and to establish a long-distance footpath beside the Ribble from its source to the sea. This is now 'The Ribble Way'.

I thoroughly enjoyed taking part in these struggles. Alan Howard succeeded me as Group Chairman of the Preston and Fylde Group. Returning to live in Sheffield I was Assistant Secretary to dear Noel Norton in 1973 and 1974 and Area Secretary from 1975 to 1980. Prior to 1974 the Area stretched from Edale to Goole, and from north of Barnsley far down into Derbyshire, there being no Derbyshire Area at the time.

My paper to reorganise the Sheffield and District Area into the present South Yorkshire and North East Derbyshire (SYNED) boundaries was eventually accepted. This was done to make our RA (SYNED) boundaries exactly fit the new Local

Government areas which came into being on April 1, 1974, thus making our footpath work and membership territory match-in with the new set-up.

Working with me were two excellent chairmen: first, Ernest Wilkinson, and then Walter Grocock. There were also a tip-top Footpaths Secretary in Jack Burling, and a most enthusiastic Access Secretary in Howard Hill. Other friends, too numerous to mention, in and beyond Sheffield during this period, made the burden of work light, if time-consuming.

As the Area Careers Officer for the High Peak and Derbyshire Dales I was fortunate enough to spend the last 13 years of my working life (1977-90) every day in the Peak District, as I had to travel all over an area between Glossop and Sudbury, and between the Derwent and the Dove - and I got paid for it!

Since then I have had a few years on the Sheffield Group Committee and later on the Area Access Sub-Committee. An invitation to be on the Branch Executive Committee for the Council for the Protection of Rural England (CPRE) was accepted, and I am also a member of the Sheffield Campaign for Access to Moorland.

The freedom of an Englishman to walk without let or hindrance over his own native hills has always been so very important to me. Slogging it out 'over there' in the war, I kept G.H.B. Ward's *Clarion Ramblers' Handbooks* ALWAYS in my pocket - and our moorlands firmly in my mind.

Clarion Handbooks

Remembering 'Jock' Byford

by Roy Bullen

When I got demobbed and came home in September 1947, I started rambling, and one of my best friends was Derek Goodwin, who later emigrated to Canada, Australia and finally New Zealand, where he now lives. Derek had joined the Barnsley Mountaineering Club (BMC) when I was overseas and so had some other young people from Sheffield. One was Jock Byford - nobody I knew called him Jim.

Derek took me a few times to the house where Jock lived with his parents. It was opposite the tram sheds on Holme Lane, Malin Bridge. Jock used to have friends round the house on occasional evenings to hear Scottish music, played on the wind-up gramophone. I believe Jock was born in Scotland of English parents when his dad went up there to work, and he certainly did have a slight accent, not local Sheffield, and at times he did wear a kilt.

The BMC did walking and climbing and held weekend 'meets'. These were often at Hope and up the Snake Pass, where the club had some overnight accommodation. At Hope it was a simple stone barn in the field next to Hope railway station, by the footpath from the footbridge up to Win Hill. Up the Snake it was at Wood Cottage, just off the A57 between Hayridge and the Snake Inn.

The BMC did most of their walks in rough country. Locally it was in the High Peak and on the Pennine moors up to and beyond Huddersfield. They didn't go so much on the limestone. Crowden and Laddow Rocks plus the Roaches and Stanage were their sort of places. On Christmas and Easter weekends I remember they went to Glencoe, Arran and North Wales. They didn't bother about access much. I can't say they actually campaigned for the right to walk freely - they just went. They assumed the freedom to roam.

Jock was one of several Sheffield lads in the BMC. I did not become a member and was only ever on the fringe - I was more Ramblers' Association and Campaign for the Protection of Rural England. But through Derek I got to know Jock. He met Doris, who was also a BMC member, and they got married in 1951.

Jock got the tenancy of one of the Woodland premises up the Snake Pass. The landlord was the Duke of Devonshire. Over the years Jock and Doris improved the old place, and Doris still continued to live there after Jock's death. They had two children, Andrew and Sheena. Besides being a good rambler and out-of-doors man, Jock was an exceptionally good cricketer. He even played for Sheffield United Cricket Club as an off-spin bowler, and later he played for Bradfield Cricket Club, even when he lived up the Snake.

He worked, I believe, as a plumber for Sheffield City Council and travelled to work for a while on a motorbike. Later on he cut his mileage to work by getting a post as the roadman for the Snake Road. Living in the wilds he did not go with the BMC so much anymore.

His politics were left wing and he was well-read and well-informed on all Labour Party matters. He could inject politics into a discussion on almost any other subject, but not in a strident way; he was more persuasive and quietly spoken. I used to go over the Snake Pass a lot in the late 1960s and through the 1970s. I used to stop the car when I saw Jock at work on the road, cleaning blocked drains and gullies and shifting debris that the rains had washed onto the road. We would have a chat for 20 or 30 minutes.

Jock's children went from the age of 11 onwards to the local secondary school, which was not very local at all - Hope Valley College. In time Jock got more into the local Woodlands politics and he thus became a governor at the school. In March 1985, a few months after he died, there was a special evening at Hope Valley College which a good number of people attended, including me and my wife Pat. Jock was very well thought of in the area.

His booklet, *Moorland Heritage*, records much about the Snake and Hope Woodlands which would otherwise have been forgotten. He did not think at all badly of his own landlord, the Duke (of Devonshire), and his career took another turn after he gained educational qualifications which got him a new job as a lecturer at the Myers Grove Further Education Unit at Malin Bridge and Stannington. All these jobs involved travelling, and I believe he at some stage got a car to replace the motorbike. I went to his place on several occasions with Derek before the latter emigrated, and I have occasionally kept Derek and Doris informed about how each of them are faring.

The Snake Inn 1890

Moorland Heritage

by James S. Byford

Jock died after a short illness in October 1984. At the special memorial evening there were very many folk from the local Labour Party, Benny Rothman, Lockerbrook, various parish councils, local history groups, Agricultural Workers' Union, Peak Park Joint Planning Board (as it was then called) and so on. Jock had been chairman of the Hope Valley Labour Party and chairman of the Governors of Hope Valley College, plus other local bodies. A tree was planted in his memory in the Hope Valley College grounds in March 1985.

'Jock' Byford's classic
Moorland Heritage.

21

From Woodcraft to SCAM

by Terry Howard

Wharncliffe Crags, the Dragon's Den, Wharncliffe Chase, Grenowoods and other ancient woodlands to the north of Sheffield were my childhood adventure playgrounds. They were the 'wild' places where my father took me and my brother John on regular expeditions in search of treasure. We would make dens, explore caves, and trek through the rocky and wooded landscape. One of the magic moments was making tea in a battered old coffee pot on our methylated spirits picnic stove. The smell of the spirits, mixed with the smell of singed grass around the stove, created an aroma that still conjures up memories of those early days in the ancient oak woodlands. We never discovered any treasure, but perhaps the real treasure was just being there.

On several occasions we left our home on the Parson Cross council estate to head for the highest hill in South Yorkshire, Margery Hill, way out on the moors. As this hill shared my mother's forename it seemed an appropriate destination. The battered old coffee pot and stove accompanied us, but we never managed to get any further than Wharncliffe Woods. Margery Hill seemed elusive - a hill too far. We didn't reach it until our later teenage years.

We joined the Woodcraft Folk, an outdoor Co-operative youth movement based on the philosophy of Ernest Thompson Seton, a writer and naturalist of the late nineteenth and early twentieth centuries. He believed that the youth of the world would benefit from skills learned in the open air and close to nature.

The Sheffield branch of the Woodcraft Folk started in 1929 on what was then a trespass walk below Stanage Edge. There, several young people from the Independent Labour Party committed their lives to the ideals of Woodcraft, and the site is now known to Woodcraft Folk as 'The Rock of Resolution'.

Rock carvings on Margery Stones. (Terry Howard)

We spent many years in the Woodcraft Folk, rambling, camping, bivouacking, hostelling, never having a Sunday at home. 'Home' seemed to be the outdoors. Our leader and mentor was Basil Rawson, known to us as 'Brown Eagle'. He told us of the early years of the Woodcraft Folk in Sheffield, the anti-fascist rallies and the campaigns for access to mountain and moorland. From him I learned about the 1932 Kinder Mass Trespass, the Abbey Brook Trespass in the same year, and the mass ramblers' rallies in the Winnats Pass

Stone head carving near Wet Stones, Howden Moor. (Terry Howard)

and Cave Dale. I learned later in my life that my mother had been a participant on these early mass rallies.

Learning about these access rallies cemented in my mind the inequalities in our society and the restrictions on our freedoms. I first became aware of what 'Private Land' meant on my childhood rambles on Wharncliffe Chase, not being able to explore legally the open country there. I soon realised what 'trespass' meant – I was assaulted on two occasions by farmers who didn't want me wandering off footpaths.

In later years it made me think more of what my father said about the access situation. He spent 16 years in the armed forces, six of those in the Second World War fighting for the freedoms of his country. Yet in the 1950s he could only look from a distance at the land he had fought for but was not allowed to walk on. My Woodcraft life throughout the 1950s and 1960s mapped out my future of campaigning for the right to roam over our mountains and moorlands.

When the opportunity to walk to Margery Hill eventually came, my brother and I decided on a weekend trek to walk the moors, staying at Lockerbrook Farm, the Woodcraft Folk's outdoor activity centre overlooking the Upper Derwent Valley. We walked up the Ewden Valley, heading for Bar Dike at the start of the Duke of Norfolk's Road. The 1932 mass trespass, in which the Woodcraft Folk participated, began here and went over to Abbey Brook. We walked along the Duke's Road, by now a public right of way, and we made for Flint Hill.

As we walked, the weather deteriorated rapidly. What began as a light shower of rain turned into heavy snow. As we left Flint Hill and crossed the open moor, the snow became knee deep. We fixed a compass bearing, as we could not see far in front. Experienced walkers know the difficulty in the best of conditions on Broomhead Moor and Upper Commons. As we walked, the snow got deeper and deeper, with thick heather and peat groughs adding to the difficulty. Eventually we could make out some rocks, which turned out to be Margery Stones. At last we had reached our mother's namesake - but by now we were in the midst of a blizzard, with the rocks covered in ice.

We dropped into the Derwent Valley and within minutes we were walking in a completely different world. The grass was green and the weather mild. We headed for Lockerbrook, where we enjoyed a hot meal and a well-earned rest. Looking back on this walk and reflecting on it, I'd say we had crossed one of the most difficult moorlands in the worst of conditions. It was a challenge for our youth. Youth always needs a challenge and Broomhead Moor gave us ours.

Another carving, near Wet Stones. (Terry Howard)

In 1982 I was one of the founder members of Sheffield Campaign for Access to Moorland (SCAM), representing the Woodcraft Folk and carrying on their traditions. As the leader of the teenage group, the Ventures, I supported all the early SCAM trespass walks and events. I believed at the time, and I still do, that access to moorland is more than just demanding a right for its own sake.

We had to demonstrate why we wanted that right and its importance for everyone. Healthy exercise, fresh air, being out together with others, sharing experiences, making new friends, the physical challenge, the opportunity to achieve and succeed, the chance to escape city life for quiet contemplation and reflection, the opportunity for creativity, the educational enjoyment of our cultural heritage and wildlife - all these reasons were put forward by the early access campaigners.

When I became SCAM's Access Secretary, I endeavoured to make all our trespass and campaigning activities reflect these same reasons. I believed we should always remain firm and consistent but at the same time responsible in everything we did. We never compromised the principle of access to open country but always remained willing to talk to and engage with landowners. We had to be seen as a responsible campaigning body and in that I believe we achieved our objectives. We attracted and generated much positive publicity. Although we were never a 'mass' organisation, we were determined enough to make our modest membership into a credible campaigning organisation.

Our resolve to succeed has paid off. We now have the opportunity to explore our countryside, a dream of many access campaigners. SCAM has firmly earned its place in the history of access.

How I Got Involved in SCAM

by Dave Chellone

Sometime early in 1982, I picked up a leaflet in Sheffield advertising a forthcoming public meeting. The purpose of this meeting was to solicit support for a local group to complement a Manchester-based committee which was planning the celebrations to mark the 50th Anniversary of the Kinder Mass Trespass of 1932.

I realised that this group would combine two of my interests: vaguely lefty activism and walking (occasionally trespassing) on the hills and moors. I involved myself with what soon became the Sheffield Organising Committee, which later evolved into the Sheffield Campaign for Access to Moorland (SCAM).

I was elected to the post of SCAM Treasurer at the AGM in 1988, and, as is sometimes the case in organisations like ours, I have been re-elected, unopposed, ever since.

The Bamford Edge mass trespass sets off across the forbidden moor on March 28, 1982. (Terry Howard)

Bamford Moor - SCAM's First Mass Trespass

by Dave Chellone

Bamford Moor was chosen as the venue for SCAM's first mass trespass, which took place on Sunday, March 28, 1982. This moor had the distinction of being an interesting piece of open moorland stretching from Stanage Edge westwards towards the Ladybower Reservoir, with a prominent edge – Bamford Edge – giving fine views over the reservoir. However it was and is private land, owned by Jeremy Archdale of the Sharrow Snuff Mills family, and it has only one public right of way, part of the old Penistone-Hathersage bridle road, which crosses the moor from Stanage Edge to an old quarry site near to Bamford New Road.

Hordron stone circle on Bamford Moor. (Terry Howard)

As this was probably the first mass trespass for some considerable time, there was some concern as to whether we would face any opposition, from Mr Archdale and his gamekeepers or from the police. Being arrested was seen as a distinct possibility, and leaflets were circulated beforehand giving details as to the law as it could be applied to the trespass and what to do in the event of being apprehended. The meeting point for the trespassers was an old lay-by on the A57 Snake Road, just west of the junction with Strines Lane End and east of the Cutthroat Bridge lay-by.

As we assembled we were accompanied by representatives of the media, including TV camera crews. South Yorkshire Police also turned up and officers noted down car registration numbers 'in case there was any criminal damage'. The only criminal damage we could envisage was damage to our cars by local hoodlums. I recall that Jack Burling thought this was a possibility and he volunteered to remain in the lay-by to try to prevent any vandalism.

Our plan had been to climb a locked gate near to the lay-by to get onto the moor, but, surprise, surprise, the gate had been mysteriously unlocked for us. Taking advantage of this some 300 plus trespassers (350 according to the next day's issue of *The Guardian*) streamed onto the private moor and we made our way in fine but windy weather to our first stop, the Hordron stone circle overlooking Jarvis Clough.

We continued to the shooting shelter towards the head of Jarvis Clough and then over rough ground to Bamford Edge itself, where our lunch stop had been scheduled.

The edge had long been popular with climbers, but they had always had to seek permission from Mr Archdale in order to avoid being harassed by his gamekeeper, Mr Darwent. Apparently he was in the habit of letting about six climbers on the crags at any one time. It turned out that on the day of the SCAM trespass, a party of 27 from the Castle Mountaineering Club were climbing on the edge, and as they came over the top, they came face-to-face with the SCAM trespassers eating their butties.

At no time did we meet any opposition, and it was later rumoured that the police had advised Mr Archdale and his gamekeeper to go out for the day and try to ignore the event. It is highly likely that they opened the gate onto the moor to avoid it being damaged, and if that was the case, it was nice of them to be so considerate. The press and TV gave us a fair amount of coverage, in spite of there not being any blood on the heather. The success of the event gave us all a lot of encouragement to make the Kinder 50th anniversary celebrations an even bigger occasion and, of course, to continue a programme of trespasses on the other private moorlands to the west of Sheffield.

Some dissent did appear in print however. John Blackhurst, Secretary of the Derbyshire branch of the National Farmers' Union was quoted in the Sheffield *Star* as writing in the NFU magazine: 'It is a tragedy that a new breed of people appears to be clamouring for a greater share of the countryside. They are hard-nosed agitators

Some Features of Bamford Moor

There are two stone circles on the moor (including the one at Hordron visited on the March 1982 trespass, at GR SK 215868), and there are cairn groups (probably ancient burial sites). The OS map also mentions enclosures, hut circles and a field system, all of which provide evidence of occupation of the moors since the Bronze Age.

Another ancient bridle road known as the Bamford Wood Gate crosses the moor and can be followed from the access point at the south eastern edge of the Heatherdene car park. This track leads over Bamford Edge, crosses Jarvis Clough near the shooting cabin and heads towards Moscar. It is thought that this is part of a packhorse route which linked Bamford with Bradfield or Penistone.

There are two stone-built pillars near to GR SK 208860, which are believed to be part of the western survey tower erected for obtaining the correct alignment for the tunnel which conveys water from the Ladybower to the Rivelin Reservoirs.

determined to break into the social fabric of rural areas built up over many generations. Their aims are not for the general public - they are very much more sinister'.

SCAM has revisited Bamford Moor several times over the years and on one trespass found Mr Archdale and some of his staff waiting at the shooting cabin. As on almost every occasion when SCAM met representatives of the land owner, the conversation that ensued was civil and usually ended with the land owner, in this case Mr Archdale, sending us on our way and wishing us well.

On Rambling and Sword Dancing

by Les Seaman

Having been born into a family that was steeped in outdoor activities, mainly cycling and the Youth Hostels Association, it is no surprise that my childhood involved being on a bike or in a hostel nearly every weekend and on holidays.

My mother had been involved in the 1930s access movement with her brother and the Sheffield Clarion Ramblers, but when she met my father, a keen cyclist, her outdoor activities moved in the same direction, and when they had a family we all took up cycling and the YHA. I was seven years old in 1944 when we stayed at the youth hostel which was then at Leam Hall near Hathersage. The war was still on, the blackout was still in place, and this was the start of an association with the YHA which was to last a lifetime, both for my parents and myself.

In 1947 came the Big Snow, and cycling was curtailed because of impassable roads, so we as a family took up walking to the hostels, mostly in the Peak District and the Yorkshire Dales. From then on we varied our weekends between cycling and walking. Before that, we had attended the Cave Dale Access Rally on June 30, 1946, which started me on a path of involvement in matters relating to rambling and the open countryside. During the next 20 years, my thinking and dedication towards moorland walking was greatly influenced by such people as Frank Turton, president of the Sheffield YHA, and Tom Tomlinson, then Warden at Rowland Cote Youth Hostel in Edale, and later first full-time Peak Park ranger.

It was inevitable that when the access movement was revived in 1982 with the formation of SCAM, I should become an active member of the organisation and ultimately its chairman.

The Sheffield Folk Club connection

In the 1970s and 1980s there was an active and lively folk club, the 'Hefts and Blades Folk Dance and Song Club', based at the Highcliffe Hotel in Greystones, Sheffield. This Sunday night club was organised by volunteers, and its membership was made up of people from various interest groups.

These included local Morris and Sword-Dancing clubs, other folk singing clubs, and a good representation of people from the higher education institutions of Sheffield, such as Sheffield University, Sheffield Polytechnic and the further education establishments. The outdoor activity movement also had good representation - walkers, climbers and cyclists - and the politics were generally left of centre and attracted many active members of Sheffield's radical movements.

When it was announced at the 'Blades' that there was to be a mass trespass on Bamford Moor on Sunday, March 28, 1982, just about the entire membership of the club turned out, and some of those members are still active in the access movement.

Rambling on Foot and in Print

by Stephen McClarence

I owe two quite separate things to SCAM. The first is the supply of good subjects for the daily column I wrote in the Sheffield *Star* from 1981 to 1994. Every other week, I would be rambling, on foot or in print. The second and more lasting thing is the way SCAM opened my eyes to the Peak District.

Before I met Terry Howard, Dave Sissons, Roy Bullen, John Harker and all the other Scammers, I was what you might term a 'lapsed walker'. Family history, perhaps touched by a little family legend, had it that my mother's father, John Arthur Rowley, was a founder member of the Clarion Ramblers. Whether or not, he sold the *Clarion*, the Socialist newspaper, on the streets of Attercliffe before his early death in the 1920s.

My mother inherited his love of rambling, and while my father was away during the Second World War, she went walking every weekend with her friend Elsie Reaney. She noted the walks in her diary: 16 miles one Sunday, 23 the next; train out, train back; tough walks, sometimes on Kinder. "When you were up on the top of Kinder, you thought you were in heaven," she said.

During my Sheffield childhood, we had a dog-eared copy of John Derry's *Across the Derbyshire Moors* with its tantalising headings ('A Wonder Walk Around Win Hill') and its adverts for 'camp clothing' ('shorts, cream cycle jackets and stockings') which were then untinged by innuendo or ambiguity. We didn't, however, run to the *Clarion Ramblers' Handbook*, that icon of walking-with-attitude, as we took our modest Derbyshire strolls and I discovered that Forge Dam wasn't the edge of the known world.

The modest walking lasted into my twenties. I never joined the ranks of ramblers who carry half their homes in their rucksacks, though I had a lingering suspicion that there must be more interesting places to walk than the well-trodden ways around Castleton and Hope.

On the evening of August 12, 1987, I finally found one of them thanks to SCAM, which, as I wrote, 'sounds a bit violent as an acronym, but these are men and women who warm to the burbling of a curlew.' That evening, with the grouse shooters' shots presumably ringing in the air, I joined the 'Walk on the Wild Side', SCAM's nifty title for its Mass Trespass across Big Moor, 'that great high tract of purple heather and scrub that spreads itself desolately, Derbyshirely, south from Fox House to Curbar'.

I called it a Mass Trespass but, as I wrote, 'SCAM insist that they are not trespassing. They have a right to be there, they say.' I remember badgering Terry Howard about this, then and on subsequent walks.

"Is this illegal?" I asked. "Can we be prosecuted?"

"Well," Terry would say, with masterly diversionary tactics, "the position is… oh look, there's a pheasant over there. The thing is, Steve, that rambling gives you open space to think. It's a necessary part of life, a spiritual thing."

And that was about as legally explicit as it ever got.

There was, as it happens, no confrontation with wardens or gamekeepers; just a couple of belligerent sheep and squadrons of flies. And revelation. Gloriously, I discovered a wholly new sense of the unimpeded space and majesty of the open moor as the sun went down and the shadows lengthened and the surrounding hills dissolved in the grey evening mist.

Discovering that was the second thing I owe to SCAM. It was a visionary moment that awoke dormant feelings about the need to walk, as often as possible, in country as wild as possible. Wet Slack Ridge and Brogging Moss, uncompromising names for uncompromising places, moved instantly up the priority list.

Since then, there have been many other trespasses and commemorations, toasted with Thermos tea, including one for an anniversary of the 1932 Kinder Mass Trespass. Pinpointed as a journalist, I was approached by an ambitious Labour politician, now less obscure than most in the government, who was desperate to get some publicity for herself. "Would you like to interview me? Would you like some quotes?" she begged. "No, not really", I said, with an honesty inspired by the open air. And I thought my grandfather, selling the *Clarion* on the streets of Attercliffe, would probably have been proud of me.

Now the Right to Roam has been achieved. Shortly after the legislation came through, I took myself off on a walk round Hathersage. I had tramped the area dozens of times, thought I knew every dip in every ditch, but on the stretch of road that scrambles down from Stanage to Hathersage, I suddenly came across a new and unexpected gate in the wall.

A little matchstick man, the symbol of access, was up there on a sign, looking somewhere between an alien and the figure indicating a Gents toilet. He beckoned a new way over the moor and I followed the guideposts up through the heather to the craggy rocks at the top. And as I climbed, a new view edged over the brow. It was more liberating than I could have hoped: a sweeping panorama of Hathersage village, which I've known all my life but was now seeing from a completely new angle. It nestled in the valley bottom, with the sun behind the trees casting long shadows down the flanking hills. It was a marvellous moment, a tribute to years of access campaigning – and it's the third thing I owe to SCAM.

Alias George Samuels

by Roly Smith

I think I first became aware of the existence of the group that became SCAM in April, 1982, at the 50th Anniversary celebrations of the Kinder Scout Mass Trespass at Hayfield. At the time, I was a feature writer on the *Birmingham Post & Mail*, and it was the first time that I met Benny Rothman and a number of the other original trespassers and access campaigners.

I was desperate to find a Midland connection so that I could cover the event, and I remember the relief when I discovered that Benny's son, Harry, was then a lecturer at Birmingham's Aston University. That meant I could legitimately write about the event in the *Evening Mail*.

As a keen walker and outdoor journalist, I had always been fascinated by the access battles of the 1930s and later, and researched and wrote about it at every available opportunity. I'd got to know and respect people like my mentor Tom Stephenson, and one of my fondest memories is walking with him along a section of his lasting legacy of the Pennine Way in 1976.

I was also interested in the Red Rope connections, and this was renewed at the 60th Celebrations in 1992, by which time I was working as Head of Information Services with the Peak District National Park. By then, I'd also got to know Stephen Morton, Roy Bullen, Jack Burling, John and Irene Bunting and Terry Howard quite well, and a feature I wrote about the anniversary for *The Great Outdoors* won the Outdoor Writers' Guild feature award that year.

As part of the National Parks Awareness Campaign (1984-87), I'd managed to persuade Benny Rothman and Tom Stephenson to speak from the same platform (something which, because of their mutual antagonism, they'd never done before) at an access rally which I organised in Cave Dale, Castleton, in June 1986.

Another speaker was Stephen Morton, a leading member of the RA, a former National Park Board member, and an organiser of some of the famous access rallies which had taken place in Cave Dale and The Winnats in the 1930s and 40s, which I was trying to replicate. He was ill, old and frail, I remember, and had just returned from a holiday in Spain, but he galvanised the crowd of 1,000 people by telling them that the war has not been won, even though the first stage – the creation of National Parks – had been achieved.

He pointed out that although the Peak Park had done more than anyone else in the cause of access through agreement, even it had fallen short. "They have fallen short of what we want because with all the goodwill in the world, you can't buy agreements if you have no money to buy them."

Of course, as an officer of the National Park, I'd had dealings with SCAM, and remember being warned off about speaking to them in my official capacity. That never stopped me talking to Terry and Roy, whose charming anthologies about rambling I always thought were worthy successors to G.H.B. Ward's classic and avidly-collected *Clarion* handbooks. (In a later life, I was delighted to be able to publish SCAM member Dave Sissons' *Best of the Sheffield Clarion Ramblers' Handbooks* for Halsgrove in 2002.)

But it was when SCAM came out with *Freedom of the Moors* - a book of 'alternative' (i.e. trespass) rambles in the Peak District, in 1988 - that I first really realised what good work SCAM had been doing over the years. I was desperately keen to review what I considered to be an important publication in the best traditions of Peak District trespassing, but knew that I would be in trouble if I was seen to be doing so as an officer of the Park.

That was why, for the first time ever, I used a *nom-de-plume*, choosing my two middle names to create 'George Samuels', as the reviewer's name appeared in *The Great Outdoors* (now *TGO*). In that review, I said that since the creation of the National Park in 1951, the Peak had negotiated many access agreements with landowners on the former battlegrounds of the 1930s, and that 56 per cent of the national total of access land was still to be found in the Peak.

'But even here, less than half the open countryside is covered by such agreements, and progress in extending public rights of access have been almost non-existent in the past 30 years. That is the reason for this booklet of alternative rambles in the Peak District, compiled by SCAM and based on routes used on their regular mass trespass demonstrations.'

Later on with Terry, SCAM members and others, I helped to organise the 70th Anniversary Celebrations of the Kinder Trespass in April 2002 - an event which will always be remembered for the immensely dignified apology by the late Duke of Devonshire for the actions of landowners in the Thirties. I also made sure that the programme included an account of the 'Forgotten Trespass' by Sheffield ramblers and Woodcraft Folk on the Duke of Norfolk's Road in August, 1932, five months after the better-known Hayfield one (see pages 36/37).

And I was delighted to hear that after the enactment of the CROW Act in 2004, SCAM had held a meeting and agreed, just as Stephen Morton had nearly 20 years before, that although a hard-fought and long-running battle had been won, the war was not yet over.

Although it is a matter of great regret to me that people like Benny, Tom and Stephen were not here to witness it, partial freedom to roam is at last with us. And I have no hesitation in saying that no group, official or otherwise, did more than SCAM to achieve that Holy Grail of the rambling and outdoor movement. Anyone who now enjoys their birthright of that cherished freedom to roam owes a big 'thank you' to SCAM.

The Shock of the New

by Dave Sissons

In 1988 I was working in the Graves Art Gallery Office above Sheffield's Central Library. For a brief period the library had a shop in the foyer selling local publications, and it was there during the summer of 1988 that I came across the newly-published SCAM booklet, *Freedom of the Moors*. At the time I was cycling solo a lot into the Peak District and going on longish walks with colleagues from work, often revisiting places I'd been to on regular family Sunday outings during childhood in Rotherham.

Twenty years previously I'd been on the anti-Vietnam War demonstration in Grosvenor Square in March 1968, and when I later went to a college in North East London I became a member of the International Socialists. I lapsed after two years, and though I never rejoined I occasionally attended public meetings when the organisation was, from 1977, called the Socialist Workers' Party (SWP). Sometimes I even had letters and news published in the organisation's newspaper, *Socialist Worker*, and I generally hovered around the fringe for years.

Meanwhile in 1974 I'd moved from London to Sheffield, and from 1975 to 1980 I spent a lot of my free time going 'back to the land', first working on commercial farms in Kent, but then working on self-sufficient organic smallholdings in various parts of the UK and Eire. I tried to get involved in the setting up of Heeley City Farm in Sheffield in 1981, but the meetings tended to drive away all but a clique of local Labour Party activists.

As the 1980s wore on I found it increasingly difficult to stay detached from politics, finding Tory Government policies a bit like classical Marxism in reverse, and during the 1984-85 miners' strike I became involved through library SWP members in a miners' support group which focussed on Barnborough pit near Mexborough. When I read *Freedom of the Moors* in 1988 it was just what I was looking for - left-wing political *and* country. I got in touch with SCAM, speaking on the phone to the Secretary, Terry Howard, and for the first time in over 16 years, I became a paid-up member of a political organisation.

Even then I did nothing for two years. I was no committee man, usually finding business meetings boring, and I was wary of spending precious free time on SCAM rambles with people I didn't know. But later in 1988 I bumped into John Widdowson, who ran Sheffield University's Centre for English Cultural Tradition and Language (CECTAL). I'd done a CECTAL course from 1982-84, and I'd heard of a marvellous new MA course (Local History, Literature and Cultural Tradition) which the centre had started running in 1987. I asked John for details and was soon enrolled onto the two-year course, starting in October 1989.

34

In the early summer of 1990 I had to decide on a dissertation subject, and one of the tutors, David Hey, suggested the Sheffield rambler, G.H.B. Ward, who had founded the Sheffield Clarion Ramblers and edited the Sheffield Clarion Ramblers' booklets, from their inception as prospectuses in 1902 until his death in 1957. Reading the booklets made me think again about SCAM.

I attended my first SCAM ramble on Sunday, August 12, 1990 - a trespass ramble on Bamford Moor, visiting the Hordron stone circle, Bamford Edge and the long-demolished Old Woman Stone. Over the summer the moors had been dry and inflammable, and the Peak National Park Authority had imposed a general access ban, but suddenly this had been lifted in time for the Glorious Twelfth, despite little rain.

There were 18 of us on the trespass ramble, including a baby. The leader was Rob Wilson, who had co-written a booklet called *Strange Sheffield* and was currently writing one on springs and wells in the Sheffield region. There was Stuart Brennan, whom I'd worked with at the end of 1974, surveying public transport usage for the new South Yorkshire County Council. There was Ian Wallace, an SWP member who I'd often seen and chatted to at Nether Edge crossroads where he regularly sold *Socialist Worker* on Friday evenings. And there were John and Irene Bunting and Jack Burling, long-standing members of the RA, John having even attended access rallies in Cave Dale in the 1930s and 1940s.

I'd rarely been off footpaths before, so it felt strange to be striding across tracts of purple heather, and the effect of surveying Hope Valley from the new viewpoint of Bamford Edge reminded me of a similar feeling induced by some of the art I'd seen over the years in various galleries - the familiar seen from a fresh angle, the shock of the new. On Monday, September 10, 1990 I attended my first SCAM meeting, and I've been a regular on rambles and at meetings ever since, taking on the post of Minutes Secretary when Malcolm Dixon moved to York in 1995.

Kinder Trespass Celebrations, 1982

by Leah Fleetwood

It was at a meeting of people interested in writing that I heard about it. The announcement was probably quick and factual. But I was alerted. This future event sounded to my story-attuned ears to be about a slaying of a Monster, the winning of a Treasure. To take part involved a Journey.

With instructions scribbled down, back home I told my son what I knew. He was old enough to cope, and he wanted to come.

So we joined others and took the train to Hayfield (a rapturous ride in itself) and were guided to a pub yard - where to the celebratory vibrancy of an accordion, men were cracking staffs and leaping a jingling pattern on the cobbles.

No memory of drinks, eats; it's like a dream now. Walking out of town in a throng, a throng with reassuring vibes, a gradual climb, cheered by bright window boxes and bystanders beaming. If there is a sneering or hostile face watching the procession, I fail to see it.

Trees, beasts grazing. A Water Board sign. A quarry. Speeches. Me trying to give my son without preachiness the context to the occasion: a sense of history, the idea that you can change things for the better.

On we go: rougher vegetation, narrowing trail, the urge to touch, inhale everything, the luxury of space for breathing deeper and looking further. Kinder Downfall - resonant words and, at this point of ignorance, enigmatic. A place of water scoring down rock: the goal, the grail. (Did we actually make it that day?)

Walkers set out on the Kinder Scout Mass Trespass Anniversary, 1982. (Peak District National Park)

On the way back I murmur, "See the man in front, Paul?" He looks at the short, vigorous figure whose heels are just ahead of our toes. "That's the man!" I whisper, "who helped organise it. Only young. Gave a speech. Put in prison. Nice man. Fifty years ago." Paul feels very close to his much-thumbed *The Lord of the Rings;* does he perhaps recognise in the cheerfully chatting rambler, near enough to touch, a likeness to one of those archetypal characters seeking to overcome the Ego in pursuit of the Self? I think now, 23 years on, we were surrounded by such characters.

A crocodile of walkers ascend the Snake Path in William Clough on the 50th anniversary celebrations. (Peak District National Park)

Anyway, when I venture to mumble a greeting, Benny Rothman puts us, a couple of tenderfoot ignoramuses, at our ease, showing us a huge heart in a small, if robust, frame. Everyone we speak to, whatever shape, is like that.

Back at the quarry we talk to a woman in a wheelchair. Over the years she and her husband have walked many a muddy-booted mile together; now she must sit tight and wait for him. A terrible severance. She smiles.

Twenty-three years ago. I've not forgotten Benny (I later came to know him better – and miss him), nor that woman. The woman prevented from stretching out, breathing deeply, negotiating her way, achieving that intoxication that comes from country walking whatever (almost) the weather; the happiness that flows, chemically and magically, through the aching bones.

Twenty-three years ago. I went to see what it was all about. What was the Monster? What was the so precious Treasure? What kind of people engaged in the struggle? The nugget of understanding I was given that heartening day has led me on ever since to explore further along the trail.

Walter Grocock and the Three Bronze Plaques

by Terry Howard

Walter Grocock, a founder member of SCAM and a regular trespasser, died early in 1994. In his memory many of his friends, colleagues and comrades donated money to SCAM to be put towards a fitting tribute to him. Knowing Walter, SCAM believed he would have preferred a memorial that was dedicated not just to him but to people like him who campaigned long and hard for access to our moorland heritage.

Shortly after SCAM was formed in 1982, a tape/slide show was made, entitled *Trespassers Will Be Celebrated*. It recorded the history of the access campaign and waymarked the future of the campaign as we saw it then. For many years it did the rounds, being shown to many people and organisations to promote the case for access to moorlands. In time, it started to show signs of wear, and we decided to transfer the material onto video.

The SCAM plaque at the entrance to Sheffield Town Hall. (Dave Sissons)

It seemed appropriate that the Walter Grocock Memorial Fund might be used for this purpose. Unfortunately, after much effort in seeking video specialists, it became clear that the material could not be transferred because of its deteriorating quality. Meanwhile the year 2000 was upon us and the Countryside and Rights of Way Act was soon to be implemented. We could not allow this momentous occasion to pass, so another use for the Walter Grocock Fund was put forward - why not commemorate all past and present access campaigners by having three bronze plaques made and positioned at appropriate locations associated with the access campaign?

The idea was adopted, and Doug Hewitt, an access supporter and Ramblers' Association member, was commissioned to undertake the work. He quickly produced the mould which was used for three bronze casts, containing an image of the early and formidable access campaigner, G.H.B. Ward, addressing ramblers at one of the Winnats Pass or Cave Dale mass rallies in the 1930s or 1940s. The finished work was spectacular, and as Doug said: "It was a labour of love" - his contribution to the campaign for access to moorland.

A SCAM meeting decided on the locations of the casts: one to go either in Winnats Pass or Cave Dale near Castleton, sites of the mass rallies of the 1930s and 1940s; another to be given to the City of Sheffield in recognition for its support for the access campaign; and the last to go to the Sheffield Clarion Ramblers, who were about to celebrate their centenary in September 2000.

The snowy unveiling of the Winnats Pass plaque, December 30, 2000. (Yorkshire Post)

Plaque One was, with the support of the National Trust as landowners, fixed to an earth-fast boulder in Winnats Pass on the site of the early access rallies. It was officially unveiled in December 2000 in the presence of Sir Martin Doughty, Chair of the Peak District National Park Authority; Paddy Tipping MP; Kate Ashbrook of the Ramblers' Association National Executive, plus several Sheffield City Council members, National Trust officers and SCAM members.

Plaque Two was presented to the Lord Mayor of Sheffield, Councillor Pat Midgeley, at a civic reception held for SCAM activists. After much discussion with councillors and planning officers (the Town Hall being a Listed Building), the plaque was eventually positioned in the entrance of the Town Hall.

Plaque Three was presented to the Sheffield Clarion Ramblers at their Centenary Dinner with a suggestion that they might like to present it in turn to the Peak District National Park Authority. This they did, and it was placed along with the 1932 Kinder Mass Trespass plaque in an access display in the Information Centre at Fieldhead in Edale, and it will be included in an access display in the new 'Moors for the Future' centre at Edale.

All in all, each plaque found its way to a politically-relevant place associated with the access campaign, and we feel sure that Walter would have approved and been proud of his association with the three plaques.

ROUTES TO ROAM *(refer to maps for route details)*

WALKS ON THE WILD SIDE

By Dave Sissons, maps by Terry Howard

The souls that live in Sheffield town have heaven at their gate:
Curlew call and lark-song and streams like ale in spate,
And there, among the heather hid, the keepers lie in wait.
Nos protigat Domine.
(from *Lift Up Your Eyes* by Michael Kelly)

In June 1988 SCAM published an A5-size booklet of trespass rambles. The original title was *Walks on the Wild Side*, but this eventually became *Freedom of the Moors*, subtitled *Alternative Rambles in the Peak District*. The rambles focussed on 10 of the forbidden areas of moorland to the immediate west of Sheffield – Snailsden Moor, Thurlstone Moor, Midhope Moors, Broomhead and Bradfield Moors, Strines Moor, Hallam Moors, Bamford Moor, Eyam Moor, Gibbet and Brampton East Moors and Big Moor.

Each ramble was accompanied by a map, and an approximate route was described, including features of historical and archaeological interest. The booklet was jointly written by SCAM members, but with a lot of input from Terry Howard and Roy Bullen. The introduction to the booklet included information on safety on the moors and public transport (or the lack of it after deregulation in 1986), a reading list, a statement of SCAM's aims, a brief history of the access movement and an article on Parliamentary Enclosures (1750-1850) – *How We Lost the Moors* – contributed by Jim Byford and based on a previous leaflet.

Some of the funding for the booklet had come from the Ramblers' Association, and the Preface included a statement from Alan Mattingly, then Director of the Ramblers' Association: 'The National Executive Committee of the Ramblers' Association is pleased to give assistance to the Sheffield Campaign for Access to Moorland in their production of this booklet. The views and advice which it contains do not necessarily reflect RA policies; indeed the RA and SCAM do not always see eye to eye. However, our differences are mainly those of tactics and presentation. Our objectives are identical: we both want to encourage people to go walking in the countryside and we both want to secure a right of access on foot to all open, uncultivated moor and mountain in Britain.'

By the autumn the booklet had been ignored by most of the outdoor magazines, but it did receive a favourable review from one George Samuels, a pseudonym used by

Roly Smith, Head of Information Services for the Peak Park Planning Board at the time (see page 28).

Not everyone was as pleased as Roly by the publication of *Freedom of the Moors*. SCAM Secretary, Terry Howard, reported at a SCAM meeting on October 10, 1988 that Fitzwilliam Estates were dismayed, to say the least, that SCAM was encouraging the general public to break the law and trespass on 'private land'. Fitzwilliam Estates, based at Wentworth Woodhouse near Rotherham, own the Bradfield and Strines moors, which are the locations for two of the trespass walks in the SCAM booklet.

Terry had replied, stating SCAM's position, and the Fitzwilliam Estates land agent had written further to say that SCAM would get no co-operation towards access agreements from private landed interests if the organisation continued to advocate such policies.

ROUTE 1 - Milestones on the Road to Access

by Dave Sissons

This ramble was included in the booklet produced to mark the Kinder Scout Mass Trespass 70th Anniversary celebrations, which took place on Saturday, April 27, 2002. The route follows long-standing public rights of way and access land for which

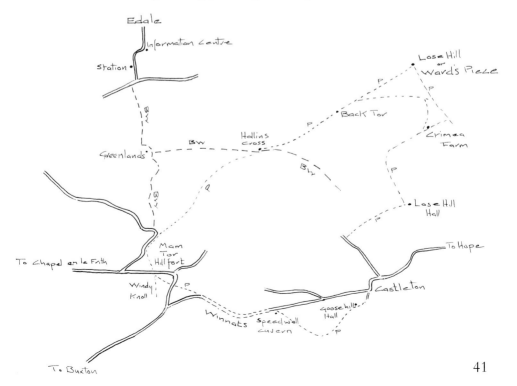

The sign to Lose Hill Pike – now changed back to Ward's Piece.

previous generations must take the credit and which present and future generations must not take for granted.

The walk starts at Castleton bus station, passing St Edmund's Church and the approach to Peak Cavern, and following the footpath behind Goosehill Hall, leading to Speedwell Cavern. About a quarter of a mile up the Winnats Pass, on the right-hand side, there is a small boulder with a plaque attached.

This plaque celebrates the 2000 CROW Act and is dedicated to walkers and ramblers who have campaigned for access over the last century or so. The plaque was sponsored by SCAM and designed by Doug Hewitt, a member of the RA. It was fixed in place during a rally in December 2000, one month after the CROW Act became law. The picture on the plaque is based on photographs of the mass rallies which took place at this very spot or in nearby Cave Dale throughout the 1930s and 1940s.

Continuing up the Winnats Pass, turn right up the footpath to Windy Knoll, and from here, climb up to Mam Tor summit.

This summit was once the site of an Iron Age hill fort, probably guarding a major trackway over the Pennines, a precursor of the present-day A625. In the 1930s and 1940s however, there was no public access to Mam Tor. Now its popularity as a viewpoint has resulted in considerable erosion, and the paths up to it have had to be paved with gritstone slabs. This shows one problem of concentrated access near honeypot areas like Castleton, especially where there is proximity to a road and parking space.

From Mam Tor, the walk follows the path down to Greenlands and continues down, turning right and then left to Edale station.

On Sunday, September 2, 1900, a group of 11 men and three women got off the morning train from Sheffield and spent a lovely late-summer day walking the 20 miles from Edale station, round - not over - Kinder Scout. They had a wonderful time, stopping off at Hayfield and the 'Snake Inn' before returning to Hope station via Hope Cross, in time for the evening train back to Sheffield.

From that day the Sheffield Clarion Ramblers, Sheffield's oldest Sunday rambling club, dates its birth, and its members continue an annual programme of rambles. In 1900 the Kinder Scout plateau was forbidden territory, a private grouse preserve jealously guarded by gamekeepers. It remained forbidden until the late 1950s, a good quarter of a century after the mass trespass of 1932, when ramblers and gamekeepers clashed violently on its slopes near William Clough. The Clarion Ramblers - especially their founder, G.H.B. Ward - were militant campaigners for access, long before and long after 1932, and the club celebrated its centenary in September 2000, just three months before the CROW Act became law.

Walk up from the station towards the Peak National Park Information Centre at Fieldhead, (soon to be the 'Moors for the Future' centre) then double back on the footpath which crosses Edale Road and climb up to Hollins Cross. Turn left and follow the Mam Tor ridge to Lose Hill Pike.

Lose Hill Pike was renamed 'Ward's Piece' in 1945 when Sheffield ramblers bought it and presented it to G.H.B. Ward (1876-1957) in appreciation of his outstanding campaigning work for access. On the north side of the summit a plaque commemorates this donation, which Ward promptly passed on to the National Trust, in whose ownership it remains.

Go down to Losehill Hall, the Peak National Park Study Centre, opened in 1972, then follow the path at the back of the Hall back to Castleton.

ROUTE 2 - The Public Private Moor

by Dave Chellone

Big Moor, a 10-square-mile area of open countryside on the western side of Sheffield, has a history of human occupation and use dating back to the Bronze Age and beyond. The moor has at least two stone circles, the site of a bronze age settlement at Swine Sty, evidence of prehistoric field systems, and many cairns. There are also significant numbers of more recent crosses, boundary markers and guide stoops.

Following the Enclosure Act the public were denied access to the moor, but agitation for public access began in the early years of the twentieth century and achieved a little progress in that the owner, the Duke of Rutland, allowed limited access to the 'drives' until 1924. However after 1924 even this concession was withdrawn. The moor is host to rare plants like the sundew, and to wildlife like the adder, one of the UK's three species of snake and the only poisonous one. During the past few decades the moor has been owned by various public bodies, but until the implementation of the 2000 CROW Act, these bodies did their best to prevent access to the open moor because of its flora and fauna and its rich heritage of archaeological sites.

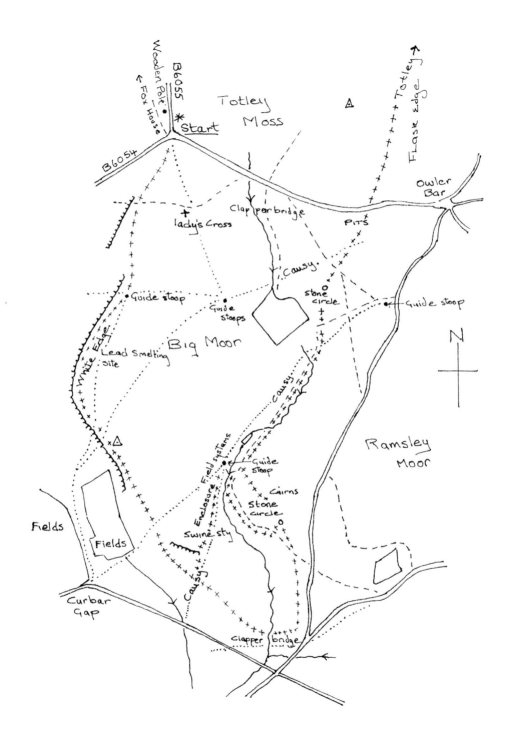

44

Recent Pressure for Access

When SCAM began in 1982, Big Moor was owned by Severn Trent Water Authority and was defended by 'Private: No Entry' signs. As such it was an early target for SCAM trespass walks and it was duly visited on December 19, 1982. As became usual for the early trespasses, the weather was atrocious, and around 40 people 'enjoyed' the day, as the SCAM minutes record, 'walking on, through and under water'. The walk served to introduce those unfamiliar with the area to the joys of walking along White Edge, with its tremendous views over the surrounding countryside - weather permitting.

In April 1983 the water authority had agreed to sell the Eastern Moors, which include Big Moor, to the Peak Park Joint Planning Board for the sum of £525,000. But the Conservative Government, in the form of Neil MacFarlane, Under Secretary for the Environment, blocked the sale because it alleged that the agreed price was below market value. SCAM's reaction to this implied threat of selling the moor into private hands was to hold further trespasses in May and October 1983, with protest meetings on the disputed land.

Nevertheless, in 1984 the moor was finally sold to the PPJPB. Under pressure from conservation groups the PPJPB's immediate reaction was to continue to have the area closed for a year while a 'study' was conducted. During this period PPJPB rangers regularly challenged walkers, particularly on the attractive White Edge. Indeed I recall an occasion when I was confronted by a ranger on White Edge who knew next to nothing about the moor and threatened to have the police meet me if I didn't obey his demand to leave the moor forthwith. I called his bluff, continued on my way and, of course, nothing happened.

The PPJPB continued with their policy, in spite of formal protests from the Ramblers' Association and SCAM, but seemed to bottle out when faced with organised and informed parties of walkers. For instance in April 1985 a 32-strong party of SCAM trespassers (in the customary foul weather) was ignored by a party of rangers encountered near Barbrook Reservoir, perhaps partly because the PPJPB had been informed in advance of SCAM's intentions.

Low Key Access?

Discussions between the RA and the PPJPB during 1985 and 1986 resulted in a form of 'low key' access agreement which was stated to be similar to one that applied to the Roaches on the south western side of the National Park. This was concluded 'at officer level' between the chair of the PPJPB, John Beadle, and the director of the RA, Alan Mattingly. The agreement seemed to involve a few footpaths, including one along White Edge, but with the main bulk of the moor being declared a 'Wildlife Sanctuary Area'. A crucial part of the agreement was that rangers would advise the public to follow designated paths (principally the one along White Edge) but would not stop anyone wandering off the paths.

This advisory and restricted role of the rangers has never, to my knowledge, been made public, and in practice rangers would have to be reminded or informed of its existence when discussions ensued on the moor. Additionally the designation of the moor as a 'Sanctuary' did not seem to mean that cattle and sheep could not be grazed there, despite the area being known to be host to rare plants.

The attitude of the PPJPB can be demonstrated by its reaction to the publicity surrounding an evening SCAM trespass on August 12, 1987. The Sheffield *Star* quoted Bill McDermott, Assistant National Park Officer, as saying that SCAM's intended route would go across a designated Wildlife Sanctuary area and that this 'would be strictly against the spirit of the agreement'.

The Situation Now

Since the implementation of the 2000 CROW Act, the whole of Big Moor, apart from a few cleared fields, has been declared Access Land. Finally, after years of resistance from many interests, both private and public, the principle of open access has been won. For that, many thanks, and now all of the moor, with its archaeological sites, wild flowers and wildlife, can be visited without fear of harassment.

ROUTE 3 - A Fluvial Peregrination

by Dave Sissons

The River Don is South Yorkshire's principal river, giving rise to the city of Sheffield and the towns of Rotherham and Doncaster, three out of four of the main urban and industrial settlements in the Metropolitan County created in 1974. Many South Yorkshire folk must at times have wondered about the source of the River Don, perhaps looking it up on a map and thinking about a visit. Yet for over a century and until September 19, 2004, there was no legal public access to the source of the River Don on Snailsden Moor.

It was not always so. Before the Woodhead line had been tunnelled under Snailsden and when grouse moors like present-day Snailsden were in their infancy, a Sheffield man had alighted from a coach at the Bordill (Bord Hill) turnpike on the south side of neighbouring Thurlstone Moor and plunged into the heather, heading north onto Snailsden in search of the source of the River Don. He was John Holland (1794-1872), son of a maker of optical instruments and born in a cottage in Sheffield Park. He explored the entire length of the River Don from Snailsden to Goole, and he wrote up his experiences and observations in a newspaper, the *Sheffield Mercury*, his articles being then gathered together to produce a book published in 1837 and titled *A Tour of the Don*.

No gamekeepers tried to turn him off Snailsden. At the time the moor was owned by John Spencer-Stanhope of Cannon Hall near Barnsley, and the moor was locally called 'Stanhope's Moor'. The nearby pub at Dunford Bridge is still called 'The Stanhope Arms', and it was formerly the Stanhopes' shooting lodge. John Spencer-Stanhope was the son of Walter Spencer-Stanhope (1749-1821), who, like a few others in various

Snailsden Pike End from near Don Well, Snailsden Moor. (Terry Howard)

Track off Windle Lane leading onto Snailsden Moor - before September 19, 2004. (Dave Chellone)

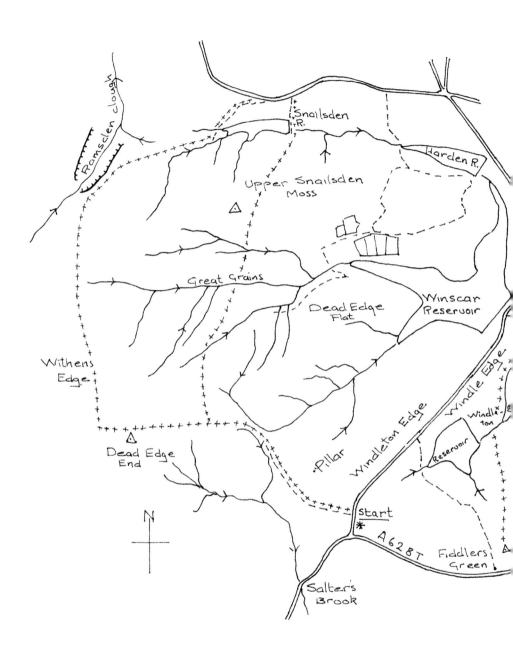

Ramsden clough

Snailsden R.

Harden R.

Upper Snailsden Moss

Great Grains

Dead Edge Flat

Winscar Reservoir

Windle Edge

Withens Edge

Windle-ton

Reservoir

Pillar

Windleton Edge

Dead Edge End

N

start

*

A628T

Fiddlers Green

Salter's Brook

48

parts of the country, was credited with the first use of grouse driving. This is supposed to have taken place near Bordill in 1805 - instead of walking with dogs after the grouse, Walter Spencer-Stanhope hid in a gully and got one of his helpers to drive the grouse over him, battue-style, which was a bit easier on the legs, for the shooter if not the driver.

This ramble can start at Bordill, near where John Holland alighted from his coach and, earlier, Walter Spencer-Stanhope lay in wait. About a mile and a half west of what used to be The Flouch Inn, on the A628, is The Dog and Partridge pub. Across the road from the pub is a track known as the Snow Road, now part of the Barnsley Boundary Walk.

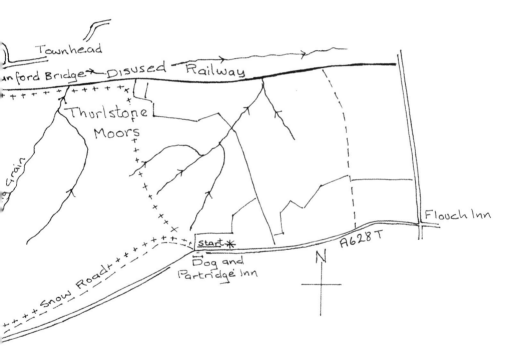

Here, on Sunday, September 29, 1991, the RA held part of its national 'Forbidden Britain Day' events, and, despite the weather being cold, wet and windy, this one turned out to be probably the most well-attended ramblers' rally since the early 1930s. The national media said the attendance figure was about 550, but the RA put it closer to 1,000. Labour MP Ann Taylor was there, as was entertainer Mike Harding, who urged everyone campaigning for access to 'go for it'. Veteran of the 1932 Kinder Mass trespass, Benny Rothman, also urged campaigners to keep lobbying the Labour Party opposition. 'And, I suppose, the Conservative Government,' he added. 'Miracles do happen.'

The Snow Road can be followed south-west for about two miles to Fiddlers' Green, where it joins another path going north-west to Windle Lane, which links Dunford Bridge to Salters' Brook and is now part of the Trans Pennine Trail. SCAM rambles on Snailsden usually began nearer the Salters' Brook end of the lane, where a track heads in a westerly direction, turning north west. This track used to be preceded by a locked gate and a sign stating: 'Private - No Road: Trespassers Will Be Prosecuted'.

On the RA 'Forbidden Britain Day' on Sunday, September 30, 1990, Benny Rothman led 50 or so ramblers over this gate and along this route onto Snailsden. The track goes over Carr Top, before forking right and narrowing to a small tussocky path which runs up the right-hand side of a stream. A brief climb leads up to the peat groughs of Upper Head Moss, from which it is a short bog-hop to the county boundary fence at Wike Head. We are standing in South Yorkshire, but on the other side of the fence is Greater Manchester, once part of a tongue of Cheshire, created when Cheshire salt magnates wanted to retain control of the trans-Pennine saltway over Woodhead into the West Riding of Yorkshire.

From Wike Head, a northerly route leads over the moor and down to Little Grain Clough, which was described in glowing terms by John Holland in the 1830s but has now been blighted by a Land Rover track and parking space created for grouse shooters. John Holland would not have approved.

In his *Tour of the Don*, he wrote, 'To an individual who, like myself, happens to be no sportsman, the solitude of these valleys is greatly relieved by the frequent rising of grouse - sometimes singly, but often several together; and, after a sort of surly note as if angry at the disturbance, alighting at a short distance among the heath: at such indications, the emotions and calculations of a true gunner would doubtless be very different from mine. During my excursion …considerable numbers of these highly-prized and beautiful birds rose and settled around me; and I must confess I felt no satisfaction in the reflection, that before three days should pass over, many a strong wing which was then clapping so vigorously would be broken, and many a dappled bosom at that moment bright and plump in the sunshine, would be ruffled and bloody through the arts of the fowler!'

Over the next ridge there are lines of grouse butts, but in the next gully flows the chattering infant Don. The Don has multiple forks west towards the watershed and its source covers a general area, though John Holland insisted that the source was Don Well, which is marked on the Ordnance Survey map. He described it as 'a hole in the bank side, apparently about twenty inches in diameter, and a dozen yards from the

A SCAM group near Don Well on Snailsden Moor. (Terry Howard)

channel of the stream, with which its beautifully pellucid water quietly mingles, after flowing down a slope deeply matted with long grass and the well-known bog-moss (sphagnum)'.

There will have been changes to the drainage of Snailsden since John Holland's time, and nothing corresponding to his graphic description of Don Well has been found, either by individuals (one using a tape measure along a stretch of the Don's north bank) or by SCAM groups. Terry Howard has suggested the most likely location for the Don Well marked on the maps, which is an area of wet flush near a line of grouse butts between the north bank of the Don and a track at the foot of Swiner Clough Moss. A south westerly route up the Don feeder groughs leads back to the County Boundary Fence at Withens Edge. The fence can be followed south to Dead Edge End trig point, which has stunning views west and east, and then back to Wike Head and the starting point.

An alternative route involves striking north at Withens Edge, but keeping a northerly direction where the boundary begins to bear west towards Britland Edge. The latter makes an impressive boundary and we can speculate whether the 'Brits' of Britland Edge were inhabitants of the Dark Age kingdom of Elmet, of which this was part of the south-western boundary. An alternative explanation was put forward by G.H.B. Ward in the *Sheffield Clarion Ramblers' Handbook* of 1914-15. He suggested there was little doubt that Britland Edge, or Bretland Edge, was named after Reginald Bretland, sergeant-at-law of Thorncliffe Hall, who died in 1708 and is buried in the chancel of Mottram church. Reginald Bretland was a benefactor to Woodhead chapel.

Eventually the route leads to Ramsden Clough, from which there are spectacular views down the Holme valley. A north-easterly direction leads to the west end of Snailsden Reservoir, from which a track progresses to the road by Cook's Study Hill. Cook's Study was a gamekeeper's tower, once set alight by a poaching gang and now a pile of rubble. Turning right along the road, which forms part of the boundary of the Peak District National Park, a track on the right leads back to the reservoir embankment, from which a south-westerly direction passes over Upper Snailsden Moss by a trig point and then over to Dead Edge End.

In John Holland's day these moors were often populous, and there was not the ubiquitous heather monoculture which currently prevails as a result of intensive grouse moor management. In his *Tour of the Don*, he wrote, 'In the months of July and August, hundreds of children, and women too, may sometimes be seen on different parts of these moors, busily engaged in gathering these minute berries (bilberries), which, possessing a sub-acid flavour, are often mixed with gooseberries in tarts: for the latter  purpose, considerable quantities are sent to Sheffield every market day during the season. Bilberries are likewise used in some of the preparations of the Manchester dye houses, the children from Holmfirth constantly collecting them for that purpose'.

As from September 19, 2004 hundreds of people can legitimately roam again on Snailsden, and like John Holland in the 1830s, we can explore the source of the Don.

Cook's Study as it was – from the cover of the Clarion Handbook 1933-34.

Left: The prostrate Old Woman stone. (Terry Howard)
Right: The Old Woman in her former glory. From Clarion Handbook 1933-34.

ROUTE 4 - Murder on the Moors

by Terry Howard

In December 1931, on the bleak and windswept moors above Bamford and Hathersage, an old woman was found murdered. She was no ordinary old woman, but 'T'Owd Woman Stooan', as local people knew her. She had been on the moors for over four thousand years, standing proud and deeply wrinkled with age. Her long presence there was a testimony to the reverence people showed to her over many generations. But now she lies broken on her death bed, covered in moss and lichens and wreathed in heather.

The old woman was a prehistoric standing stone. It originally stood over two and a half metres high, perhaps the tallest known standing stone in the Peak District, and it was heavily fluted through weathering. It would have been a very important feature in the landscape as it was used as a guide for travellers going across these moors. What a relief it must have been to have reached the stone on those wild and windswept days and to have known you were on the right way between Penistone and Hathersage. Here the ground is rutted with holloways made by travellers over the years. The stone has letters inscribed into it, one being the letter 'H', showing it was used as a boundary marker for Hathersage.

On that fateful day in December 1931, the Old Woman was felled by what appears to have been a drill or chisel. Who were the perpetrators of this crime against our

53

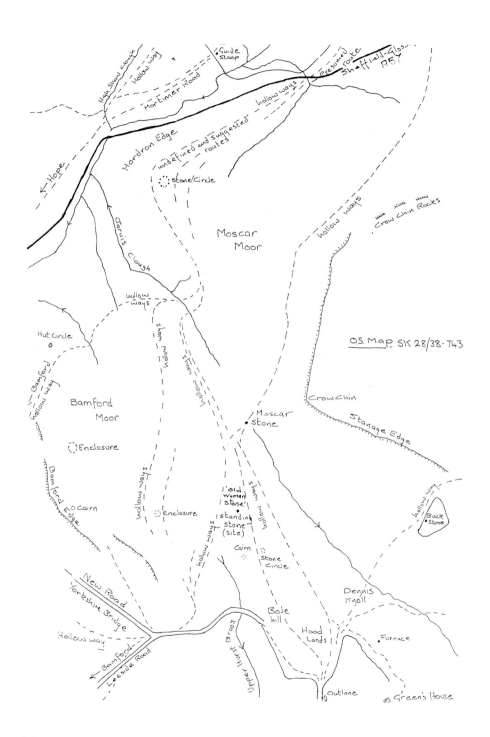

High Swin Clough
Hollow way
Guide Stoop
presumed route
Sheffield-Gloss.
A57
Mortimer Road
hollow ways
Hordron Edge
undefined and suggested routes
Hope
Jarvis Clough
stone circle
Moscar Moor
hollow ways
Crow Chin Rocks
hollow ways
Hut Circle
o
Bamford way
hollow way
Bamford Moor
OS. Map SK 28/38·743
Crow Chin
Moscar Stone
Stanage Edge
Enclosure
hollow ways
Buck Stone
hollow way
Bamford Edge
Cairn
hollow ways
Enclosure
'old woman stone'
standing stone (site)
Cairn
stone circle
Dennis Knoll
New Road
Yorkshire Bridge
Bole hill
Hood Lands
Furnace
Hollow way
Bamford - Leeside Road
Upper Hurst Brook
Outlane
to Green's House

54

heritage? Certainly not ramblers, as the Old Woman had been their guide over these moors and they had always treated her with great respect – indeed it was ramblers who reported this act of vandalism.

Although we can only guess at the original purpose of such standing stones, they are attributed with all sorts of meanings and properties. Were they simply guide stones or part of a much wider and more complex system of standing stones and stone circles? Their siting is unlikely to have been accidental – more likely they were strategically placed within a living landscape.

This old woman was mature in years and still capable of many more years of service to generations of walkers. So why was she murdered? It was because she stood on a moor which had been enclosed a century previously and the landowner did not want her to attract ramblers onto a moor they had traditionally walked over but which was now closed to them. The landowner wanted the moor for his own private use of grouse shooting. Imagine the destruction of thousands of years of respect and reverence as the Old Woman crashed to the ground! The only consolation is that the present landowner seems sympathetic to the need to conserve our heritage and may in due course help to remedy this crime allegedly perpetrated by the staff of a previous owner.

The moorlands we see looked different in the past. They were denuded of trees several thousand years ago and many man-made structures have been built on them – standing stones, stone circles, burial mounds, settlement sites, medieval crosses, causeys and the later inscribed guide stoops and milestones. Most have suffered varying degrees of vandalism, but without exception every medieval cross has been either damaged or completely destroyed. Oliver Cromwell usually gets blamed for this, but in fact many medieval crosses were still standing and were recorded just prior to the Parliamentary Enclosures of the late eighteenth and early nineteenth centuries.

As these crosses stood by the side of ancient rights of way, walkers continued to use them as waymarkers, as they had been used for centuries, even though they now stood on newly-enclosed private moorland. So from the grouse shooters' viewpoint, the crosses had to suffer the same fate as was later suffered by the Old Woman, and later still by New Cross.

ROUTE 5 - The Strange Story of New Cross

by Terry Howard

The name of New Cross has always held some intrigue for inquisitive-minded walkers. Why is there a cross in the middle of the Bradfield Moors? Doesn't a new cross imply a previous old cross?

New Cross was always a landmark on one of SCAM's favourite trespass walks. Access was via the 'New Cross Road', also known as the 'Emlin Dike Road', which starts at a gate near the junction of Windy Bank Lane with the Mortimer Road. This gate used to be left unfastened, and many walkers held the traditional belief that it was a public right of way over the moors into the Derwent Valley. Attempts were made by the Ramblers' Association to claim it as a public right of way, and as a consequence of this, and of several SCAM walks over this route, the gate was locked and barbed wire was fastened to it. Obviously the landowner did not want walkers on this old road.

The route up the track from the gate and across the moors follows two gentle dip slopes and is broken only once by a small scarp slope near a couple of shooting cabins before the long haul to Cartledge Flat. From here the route descends into the Derwent Valley, either south by Back Tor or north via the spectacular Abbey Brook, the latter being reached directly or by connection to the Duke of Norfolk's Road.

On either side of this route these formerly forbidden moorlands look inviting, challenging the curious walker to explore them. What treasures may lie hidden among the rocks and heather? But don't be deceived by this invitation in poor weather, for the inexperienced walker can experience much difficulty. What, for instance, awaits the unwary at 'Black Hole', a boggy area at the head of Hobson Moss Dike?

New Cross in winter, showing the 'sword'. (Terry Howard)

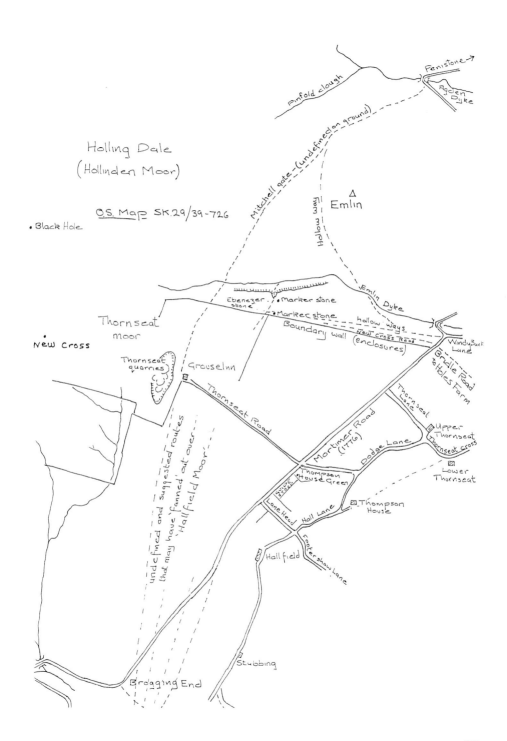

Holling Dale
(Hollinden Moor)

O.S. Map SK.29/39-726

• Black Hole

• Pinfold Clough

Mitchell gate (undefined on ground)

Hollow way

△ Emlin

Fenistone →

Agden Dyke

Emlin Dyke

Ebenezer • Marker stone
stone
• Marker stone
Boundary wall
New cross Road
(enclosures)
hollow ways

Thornseat
moor

• New Cross

Thornseat
quarries

Grouse Inn

Windy Bank
Lane

Girdle Road
to Holes Farm

Thornseat Road

Mortimer Road
(1776)

Thornseat
Lane

Upper
Thornseat
Thornseat cross

Dodge Lane

Lower
Thornseat

undefined and suggested routes
that may have 'fanned out over
'Hallfield Moor'

Thompson
House Green

Lane Head

Hall Lane

🏠 Thompson
House

Hall field

Footershaw Lane

Stubbing

Bradging End

New Cross Road was one of several lost routes over the moors into the Derwent Valley, others including Mitchell Gate from Thornseat Delf to Agden Bridge, and the Halifax Gate bridleway over Emlin Ridge, the latter being a route superceded by the Mortimer Road. Although New Cross Road seems to go only as far as New Cross, it did in effect link up with other routes at Cartledge Flat.

On the route or on adjacent ones are several standing stones, which are not prehistoric stones but more recent marker stones. The first stone reached is the Ebenezer Stone, which marks the end of the partly-surfaced and wider section. According to G.H.B. Ward in the *Sheffield Clarion Ramblers'* *Handbook* of 1924-25: 'When the men, after the (Bradfield) Enclosure Act, were marking out the boundaries of moorlands some 80 years ago, Mr Benjamin Elliott, of Smallfield Farm, after the stone was fixed, suddenly

New Cross as it was – from Clarion Handbook of 1925-26.

exclaimed - "Theer's a bit i' t'Boible, 'at says, 'Thus far shalt thou go Ebenezer and no farther'. They then threw up the bottles they had emptied and shouted hurrah, an' it's bin called Ebenezer Stooan ivver since." The quotation doubtless is wrong, but the incident shall survive'.

Beyond the Ebenezer Stone is an unsurfaced path and open moorland, where occasionally you come across a stone bearing a landowner's initials and marking a former property boundary. These stones are no earlier than the Bradfield Enclosure Award of 1826.

On reaching New Cross it will be observed that there is only the cross base and perhaps a small stone inserted into the mortice where originally a tall cross would have stood. On the cross base there is a carving of what appears to be a sword. Because the sword was a symbol used by the Knights Templars - the Knights of St. John - who held land in Bradfield, it has been suggested that this cross was one of their property boundary markers. Another suggestion which relates more to the siting of the cross is that since these moors were once known as Hawksworth Firth, this cross marks the site of 'Hawk's Worth' or 'Hawk's Settlement', though the remains of such a settlement have never been located.

My interpretation of New Cross is that it is a wayside cross on a corpse or burial road, a processional way between the outlying settlement of Holden House in the Derwent Valley, which was in the parish of Bradfield, and Bradfield Church. When people died it was customary for them to be buried in their parish churchyard, no matter how far away it was or whatever terrain had to be crossed before they reached their final resting place. Bradfield parish records show that members of the Greaves family, who lived at Holden House in the sixteenth and seventeenth centuries, were buried in Bradfield churchyard. So which way was their final journey?

I suggest that the most direct route was up Abbey Brook to Cross Hill near Cartledge Flat, then on to New Cross and down New Cross Road to the bridleway off Mortimer Road leading to Dale Road and Cross Lane. Then along Dale Road and Annet Lane to the junction with Windy Bank Lane. Another cross is recorded by Fair House Lane. Finally onto the cross at Low Bradfield (now in Bradfield Parish Church) and up to High Bradfield. The references to several 'cross' place names on this route is unlikely to be coincidental. I believe the route was one of several such processional corpse roads converging on Bradfield Parish Church from local townships or hamlets in the parish.

Although New Cross is now only a remnant, the cross shaft and cross head would have been visible from miles around, certainly a worthy guide and place of consolement for any burial party going across the moors. A lot of popish symbols were destroyed during the Reformation, but perhaps the sheer isolation of New Cross ensured its survival. However, as a magnet for ramblers exercising their right to roam on what were seen as illegally closed moors, New Cross did not survive the 1990s.

Up to then ramblers who visited New Cross would have to re-erect the broken cross shaft on its base after finding it taken down by mysterious hands, which would then mysteriously take it down again. This tussle between ramblers and presumably gamekeepers went on until one day the complete shaft disappeared. It is unlikely that a rambler carried off the shaft in his or her rucksack as it took two people to lift the shaft onto the base when it was being re-erected. More likely it was removed by gamekeepers so that ramblers would be dissuaded from visiting this highly visible waymarker on a private grouse moor. SCAM reported this act of vandalism to the Peak District National Park Authority, who contacted the landowner, Fitzwilliam Estates. The landowner of course 'knew nothing about the removal of the cross shaft'.

This walk in reverse is fairly easy from Cartledge Flat towards Bradfield via New Cross and the shooting cabins. However it is always best to use a compass bearing in case the weather changes for the worse and causes you to stray into the wrong valley or even into the 'Black Hole'.

SCAM 'STOOPS' TO CONQUER

by Dave Sissons

On Thursday, May 6, 1993 a guide stoop near Moscar House Farm was restored by SCAM to what is believed to be approximately its original position. It was erected in 1737, but sometime in the 1890s or 1910s it was moved to the gamekeeper's lodge at Strines Lane End, where, in 1913, it was photographed by Harry Inman of the Sheffield Clarion Ramblers. The founder of the Sheffield Clarion Ramblers, G.H.B. Ward, mentioned the guide stoop in the club's booklet of 1936-37, and as a result of this article, or the interest it generated, the guide stoop was mysteriously buried not far away. Ward and his associates soon found it though, and letters and articles made record of the fact. The resurrected guide stoop mysteriously moved again, this time going west, to be left prostrate by a wall where today there are some sheep pens. There it rested for the best part of 60 years. (A gamekeeper's eye-view of this dispute is recorded by gamekeeper's son, Graham Twigg, in his book, *The Keeper's Lad*, 1997.)

It was a beautiful evening on May 6, a bit cool, but otherwise sunny, breezy and very clear. A short-eared owl was quartering the moors across from

The relocation of the Strines Lane End guide post, May 1993. Right to left - Dave Sissons, Charlie Oscroft, John Harker, Steve McClarence, Leah Fleetwood. (Terry Howard)
Inset right: a close-up of the stoop from the Clarion Handbook of 1936-37.

Moscar Lodge, near the Derbyshire and South Yorkshire County Boundary, and lapwings and curlews were vociferous in the fields by the junction of Sugworth Lane and Strines Lane. Here the SCAM party assembled - Terry Howard, his son Richard Howard, Roy Bullen, Rob Wilson, Malcolm Dixon, John Roper, Shirley Meek, Charlie Oscroft, John Harker, Dave Sissons and Leah Fleetwood. Also present was the Sheffield *Star* journalist, Stephen McClarence, whose article on the event would be published in the *Star* on the following Monday. The group set off past Moscar House Farm to where the guide stoop was resting by the wall.

There was some discussion about the correct location, but after a provisional compromise was eventually agreed work began. A rope was tied round the guide stoop, and with delicate teamwork it was hauled up the field to the path, where John Harker had been busy with a spade. The guide stoop was heaved into a freshly-dug space, facing an agreed direction, and finally secured. And, though SCAM subsequently got a rap on the knuckles from the Peak National Park Authority for not consulting them first, there it still stands, roughly-carved with '1737' and giving directions to Sheffield, Penistone and Hope.

The friendly boys in blue

by Dave Chellone

It is a common complaint of the public that you can never find a policeman when you want one. The opposite of this of course is that when you don't want one you usually have no trouble finding one, and this was certainly the case on a SCAM trespass ramble of September 13, 1998. On a ramble which should not have been a police priority we twice met officers of the law.

SCAM had publicised a walk over Bradfield Moor, and while walkers were assembling on Dale Road near Low Bradfield, a car bearing a Countryside Alliance sticker kept buzzing about, and then a police car pulled up and two policemen approached the walk leader, Dave Sissons. After establishing that we were the SCAM party they informed us that the landowner, Fitzwilliam Estates, had given permission for the walk and that they (the police) had advised the local gamekeeper not to stop us. SCAM, as usual, had not actually asked for permission but simply informed Fitzwilliam Estates of our intention to walk over the moor. The police were incredibly friendly and courteous and they emphasised that with trespass being a civil offence, and currently politically sensitive, they were present to avoid possible violence 'from the other side'.

The walk began with 13 people, but two young ladies, both newcomers to SCAM rambles, obviously had second thoughts after seeing the police and they were never seen again. The rest proceeded up a bridleway to a locked gate bearing a 'Private' sign, beyond which stretched the Emlin Dike Road (sometimes called the 'New Cross Road').

A police car passed as we climbed over the gate to begin our intended trespass. Shortly afterwards we approached the two shooting cabins near Foulstone Delf (GR SK228928), and behind the window we saw a movement. We thought it was the gamekeeper lying in wait, but it turned out to be two more policemen, and we had a very friendly conversation with them while we had our elevenses.

The police told us they had no problem with people like us (respectable members of the public) but they were worried about others who might exploit the situation. Further questioning revealed that they meant hunt saboteurs or 'Swampy-type people' (this being the time of the anti-road building protests). They also said that they had been called out because of the 'politically sensitive situation' and that they were on the moor 'merely to observe'.

In fact the police had been dropped off at the cabins by the Fitzwilliam Estates gamekeeper, who had promised them a flask of coffee which was still being patiently awaited. We offered them some of ours. They enquired about our route, expressing interest in the remains of New Cross which we intended to visit. The whole encounter was so friendly that we offered them SCAM membership forms and gave them a copy of the current SCAM Newsletter. Finally they wished us well, we said our goodbyes and we went on our way.

As we ascended the gentle hill beyond the shooting cabins we looked back and saw the gamekeeper watching us from his Land Rover on the top of the opposite hillside above the shooting cabins. Nevertheless the rest of our walk proceeded as planned and without further attention from either the constabulary or the landowner's agents.

ROUTE 6 - Abbey Brook Revisited

by Dave Sissons

In November 1956 the West Riding County Council notified its decision to restore The Duke of Norfolk's Road as a public track under the 1949 National Parks and Access to the Countryside Act. Veteran rambler, G.H.B. Ward, writing in the *Sheffield Clarion Ramblers' Handbook* of 1924-25, described the track as 'the wildest Yorkshire moorland walk south of Wharfedale'. He also provided a detailed history of the track and its surrounding moorlands, specifically the loss of public rights of way and rights of access as a consequence of the Ecclesfield Tithes Act of 1811, the business of which was not concluded until 1826 at the Tontine Inn in Sheffield.

This Act had preserved two rights of way leading from Bradfield to the Derwent Valley, and one was The Duke of Norfolk's Road, but by the time Ward was writing this route was being treated as a private track from which public access was barred. Ward's article is said to have inspired the mass trespass in September 1932, in the aftermath of the Kinder Scout trespass, and nearly 40 years after the official re-opening of the track, SCAM staged a rally and ramble to commemorate this Abbey Brook Mass Trespass.

It had rained overnight in Sheffield, and the morning of Sunday, May 19, 1996 was cold, wet and grey - typical weather for a SCAM ramble, this one being part of what was then 'Sheffield Environment Fortnight'. I walked down to the 61 bus stand at Sheffield Interchange and met Terry Howard and we were soon joined by a few more SCAM members, plus Steve McClarence, a journalist previously from the Sheffield *Star* but now writing for the *Yorkshire Post*. Terry was disconsolate - it was a poor turn-out and one of the two leaders of the ramble, Charlie Oscroft, had yet to appear.

Below left: SCAM rally on Duke of Norfolk's Road, featuring original trespassers from 1932: left to right, Bill Keen, two unknown ramblers, Benny Rothman. Below right: left to right, Walter Grocock, Albert Richardson, Bill Keen. (Terry Howard)

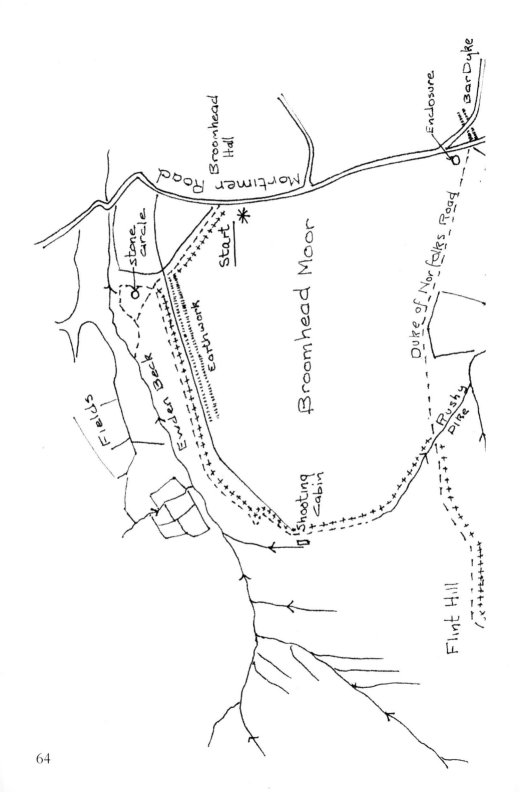

Woodcraft Folk at Bar Dike. (Terry Howard)

Only two more people joined us at High Bradfield, not including Charlie, so we set off, a mere handful. However the steady climb up to Bar Dike was quite exhilarating, and it got our blood circulating. The weather seemed to be clearing up, and I began to worry about being overclad and getting overheated, for I'd come out dressed for winter: woolly hat, gloves, scarf, thick anorak, two pairs of socks and a vest. A woodpecker was chortling from down towards Low Bradfield on our left, curlews were bubbling and gliding ahead, and some of us saw what looked like a buzzard, circling slowly, high over the moors. Terry said that ravens had been seen around Rocher Rocks, up on our right, and they had indeed returned to the Peak District in the last few years after a century or so of being relegated to place names like 'Ravens Tor'.

It had now turned into a magnificent morning: woods rinsed clean, grassy pastures lush and green, mist blowing in clouds over Emlin Ridge, raindrops sparkling everywhere. But when we reached Bar Dike there were only two more people waiting. Terry was now fed up and felt he'd been let down. BBC TV Look North had said they were coming, and the Woodcraft Folk had also promised attendance.

Suddenly Jack Burling, the other leader, appeared in the distance, leading a group of people from Low Bradfield. Then the Woodcraft Folk showed up behind Jack's group.

Then Dave Chellone pulled up in his car, carrying two of the speakers as planned, Leah Fleetwood and Bill Keen, the latter having attended the 1932 Abbey Brook Mass Trespass and now rapidly approaching his 85th birthday. There was also an unplanned presence in Dave's car - Charlie, the missing leader. He'd set off late and missed the crucial bus, but Dave happened to pass him on the Mortimer Road and gave him a lift.

We moved to the gate at the end of the Duke of Norfolk's Road. Look North at last appeared and Terry, Bill and Leah gave their speeches, during which operation the MP for Hillsborough, Helen Jackson, and some of her family turned up. Terry was now in a good mood and it showed - we were now about 35 or so, more than he had expected, and it was going to be a good day. Helen Jackson wanted to keep a low profile, but we had the promise of good media coverage from the *Yorkshire Post* and Look North. We'd been warned that the landowners had been in touch with the police about the event, and the police had certainly phoned Terry, but, as it turned out, there was no sign of opposition. There was however a push bike rally nearby, and some of the cyclists later turned out to be a nuisance.

Typed handouts had been prepared by Leah Fleetwood and Dave Sissons, and these included the memories of two ramblers who had been on the 1932 mass trespass. One was Albert Richardson (Mayor of Sheffield in 1975), who had recorded his memories for a SCAM tape/slide presentation. His testimony must have sounded familiar to Bill Keen.

'After the Kinder dispute they'd decided that they were going to hold a meeting in Sheffield to organise a protest at the activities of the police and the keepers over the Kinder ramble. There was a meeting organised in the Victoria Hall by the Ramblers' Federation, and they'd notified all the rambling clubs that this was going to happen. There were about twelve rambling clubs represented at this meeting, and we decided that we would make a mass trespass from Malin Bridge through the valley there, right over to Broomhead Moors and then to Abbey Brook.

'When we met at Malin Bridge, the press didn't know anything about it, and we didn't know whether the police or the gamekeepers did, so we walked up the Loxley Valley and over to the Brook, and when we got towards the shooting butts of Major Broomhead, we saw the police on top of the hill - there's a large hill there - and as we approached the butts they all came down the hillside. I should say there were about thirty policemen at the time and about 40 gamekeepers, and the gamekeepers had got pit shafts and the police had got dogs, and they approached us and told us we'd got to go back.

'And a colleague called Hardy, of Shipton Street Settlement, was in charge of the ramble, and he said, "If you want to stop a trespass you must escort the people onto the nearest major road. That's the ruling and the law". And the police wouldn't listen to it. They said, "No, you've got to go back". They said - they were persistent - that we must go back. And Hardy said, "Well, sit down a minute and let's talk this out". So we all sat down again. He says, "Now, are we hungry?" So we all shouted, "YES!" So he said, "Well then. Get your rucksacks off, get your flasks out, and get your grub out, and get down, and we're stopping here while we've eaten it. We're not in any hurry".

'And we followed what he said and all started eating, and the gamekeepers were getting annoyed and the police were a bit upset, and one or two of the gamekeepers started doing a bit of pushing on one or two of the lads. Well, the police stopped them and they told them they weren't having any of that. It got to be - you know - he was in charge, the police officer, and he said he'd got to see everything's in order and "We don't want that".

'But one of the gamekeepers did push one of the ILP lads, and straightaway he hit back at the gamekeeper, and hit him hard, and the police immediately grabbed them both and told them that they had got to stop. So ultimately we decided that we were walking back then. We'd go back, but we'd go at our own time and own pace and own way, and we made it as long as ever we could, and the policemen kept saying, "You know, you could cut it short a bit and be reasonable", and we said, "This is what we intend doing and we're going to do it".'

SCAM group with banner by the Duke of Norfolk's Road, February 3, 1995. Left to right, standing - John Harker, Irene Bunting, Dave Sissons, unknown, Archie Brearley behind Rob Wilson, Terry Howard behind Brian Fischer, John Bunting behind Shirley Meek. Kneeling, unknown. (Terry Howard)

SCAM group with banner on Bradfield Moor with New Cross in the foreground. Left to right - unknown, Fred Sheldon, Les Seaman, Dave Sissons, Jack Burling, Charlie Oscroft, Brian Fischer, Dave Dyson, Chris Seaman, Dave Chellone, Pat Durrant, Bev Booker. (Terry Howard)

Fast forwarding to 1996, Bill Keen gave an amusing account of the 1932 Kinder mass trespass, mentioning in particular some academic's published reference to it, which had concluded that when the Sheffield contingent on Kinder had turned round to return to Edale they had effectively 'walked out of history'. The implication of this conclusion was that if the Sheffield contingent had continued over to Hayfield, some of them might have been arrested, thereby later achieving the legendary status of the six imprisoned ramblers from the Manchester side, but as it was the Sheffield presence had apparently suffered total eclipse. Bill said that at the time it didn't feel as if they were walking out of history but rather trying to get to the Nag's Head at Edale in time for a pint before catching the train back to Sheffield!

Bill had said on previous occasions that the Kinder 1932 Mass Trespass, now legendary, had been forgotten about for 40 years, a view which ought to raise question marks about the oft-quoted contention that the Kinder Trespass led to the creation of National Parks under the 1949 Act. If it led to any legislation, the 1939 Access to Mountains Act is a more likely contender, and that Act was seen by ramblers as a landlord's charter, containing an infamous clause which criminalized trespass.

Meanwhile, in 1996, it was still a bit cold for standing around too long, so we set off down the Duke of Norfolk's Road, occasionally buzzed by bikers, some of who were polite while some were rude and downright aggressive, one lad nearly knocking Helen Jackson down. We began to straggle a bit, and Bill Keen returned with Dave Chellone to the warmth of the car. The rest of us reconvened at the Devil's Spectacles, where Terry gave another little talk. He reminded us that officially we were now trespassing, though he regarded the place as having de facto access, and anyway it wouldn't be good publicity for Fitzwilliam Estates if Helen Jackson 'got done' for trespassing in her own constituency. He also described the explanatory legends which had grown up around the Devil's Spectacles and the nearby Apron-full-of-Stones.

We moved on to the walled enclosure and the Rimington-Wilson stone, where Terry pointed out the 30 foot width of the track, a stipulation of the Bradfield Enclosure Act and Award, 1811–26. As from 1956 the track had been open to the public, but everything to the immediate north and south of the track was private and dedicated to the lucrative business of grouse-shooting. What had been commons had effectively been privatised, and in this case the eventual beneficiaries were Fitzwilliam Estates to the south and Broomhead Estates to the north.

Next halt was at Rushy Dike, where the final reading of the day was given by one of the Woodcraft Folk, a young lady called Amber. She read an extract from the diary of a

SCAM group with banner by the shooting cabin on Emlin Dike Road, Bradfield Moor. Left to right - Fred Sheldon, unknown, Dave Chellone, Les Seaman, Chris Seaman, Jack Burling, Charlie Oscroft behind Pat Durrant, Dave Sissons behind Bev Booker, Dave Dyson behind Brian Fischer. (Terry Howard)

previous Woodcraft Folk member who, at the age of 16, was another rambler who had been on the 1932 Abbey Brook Trespass (see box).

After this Terry and the Woodcraft Folk returned to Bar Dike, while Jack Burling took the lead and we straggled on to Cartledge, though a few people broke away to look at the crater on Broomhead Moor made when a plane crashed into the peat a couple of years earlier. When we found relative shelter we sat down for lunch, though Helen Jackson and family preferred to keep moving and stay warm. The main body of walkers followed Jack to Back Tor, circling round to Foulstone Delf and back to Bar Dike and Bradfield. They crossed the terrain which is featured in Barry Hines' novel, *The Gamekeeper* (1975). Researching the novel, the author had shadowed one of the Fitzwilliam Estates gamekeepers, Trevor Jones, mostly around Wentworth Woodhouse near Rotherham, but he had also attended one of the grouse shoots on this moorland.

Four of us, including Charlie, left the main party and set off down Abbey Brook. And really this was the most spectacular part of the ramble, following the narrow track down to Sheepfold Clough with Howden Chest on our right. At the ruined sheepfold the party split in half, two going back to Bar Dike, Charlie and myself continuing to the Derwent Valley. We passed the ruined shooting cabin in Cogman's Clough, but instead of sticking to Abbey Clough, we took a short cut up a faint Land Rover track and holloway to a gate and stile, then over the ruins of Bamford House and down to the Derwent Dam. This is an extremely interesting route, for it crosses a few boundary ditches and passes a cup-and-ring stone, now part of a wall near the ruins of Bamford House. We finished up at Derwent Fairholmes in time for the 257 bus back to Sheffield.

THE ABBEY BROOK TRESPASS, 1932

An extract from the diary of a 16-year-old Woodcraft Folk member who took part in the 1932 Abbey Brook Trespass.

Pleasant to see so many Woodcraft Folk ready for the mass trespass on Sunday. I think there were more Woodcrafters than anybody. We managed to get off pretty well on time and went through the Wisewood Estate, over Wadsley Common, over Kirk Edge and so on on to the top side of Bradfield for dinner. Of course we got plenty of stares as we marched along singing Woodcraft and Bolshie songs. After dinner we all set off for Smallfield, where the mass trespass was to start from. We were all told to keep together, and no names were to be mentioned.

When we arrived at the beginning of the moors, two gamekeepers were there with a man on a bike. A gamekeeper advised us to go back, and as we went straight on, he sent the cyclist with a message, we presume, to get assistance. The next part of the journey was about five miles of rough moorland, up and down tufts of grass and falling into bogs. When we got to Peter's Rock, which is a point overlooking Abbey Brook, we met with opposition in the form of about forty gamekeepers, among who were a few policemen.

Someone said that we ought to make our way down to the shooting butts, but others said we ought to carry on over the edge to Foulstone Delf. A gamekeeper was in the vicinity, and after a meeting of the Executive Committee, which all took time, we agreed to carry on, but in the meantime the gamekeepers, who we had seen in the bottom, they of course rounded up on us and stopped us, but only by the use of big pit props. Two lads got it worse than any of us, as one refused to give his name and address.

After much discussion and argument, we set off back across the way we had come, accompanied this time by the police and the gamekeepers, who kept urging us on. But they swallowed the remarks very well which we all could not resist from making, and I am sure they must have enjoyed their five mile walk on a Sunday afternoon. We shall make them ramblers yet! There was a full day of excitement, although we had to turn back, but numbers make a difference. Next time we want a thousand, not two hundred.

ROUTE 7 - South Yorkshire's Everest

by Les Seaman

It is but a short distance from the industrial valley of Stocksbridge to the wild open moorland of the Peak District; but it is a different world in atmosphere and scenery.

On leaving the water side of Underbank Reservoir, we climb via Langley Brook towards the moors north of Ewden Beck. The views to the north stretch way into West Yorkshire and beyond, and to the south is the magnificent Ewden Valley and its reservoirs, and around us are the hills to the west of Sheffield. On reaching the Mortimer Road we now cross onto open moorland by Thorpe's Brow (SK 239975) - new Access Land.

As we approach Ewden Heights, we cannot miss the relics of World War II - concrete and brick structures, targets used for firing practice by men who would then take their skills to war, fighting to save their country, the same country to which these same men would be denied access after the war by the moor owners. From these wartime relics we head up towards the east end of Earnshaw Ridge. This approach is far from easy, with its deep heather, tussocky grass and very wet bogs, and we climb all the way up to the bleached rock slabs and onto Pike Lowe.

Margaret Seaman on Pike Lowe, May 1, 2005 (Les Seaman).

Pike Lowe is 1,568ft/478 metres above sea level, and on clear days it offers some of the finest views in South Yorkshire. This large burial mound of prehistoric origin was chosen very carefully by our ancestors for its remoteness and tranquillity. On reaching this spot you feel you have achieved a personal goal, like Edmund Hillary standing on the top of Everest, or Captain Scott at the South Pole. Pike Lowe may not be the Himalayas or the Antarctic, but with all your effort, you feel you have made it to your Everest this day.

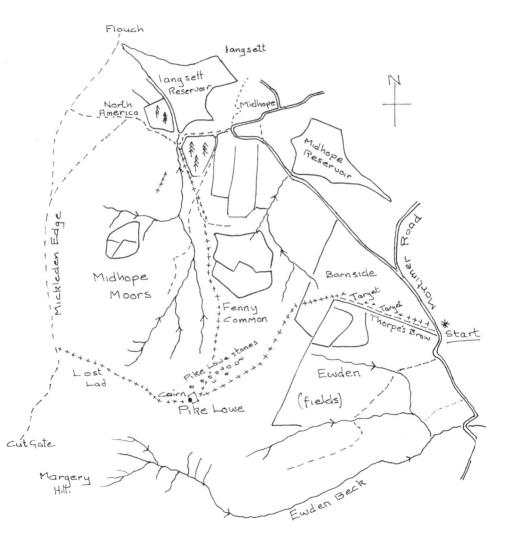

The route from the summit takes you in a westerly direction via Sugden Top towards the Cut Gate path. As we traverse this route we have extensive views across some of the remotest moorland in South Yorkshire - the upper reaches of Ewden Beck onto Margery Hill and beyond onto the hills surrounding the Upper Derwent valley. Cut Gate is an ancient track which was used by farmers in the Upper Derwent and Woodlands valleys to take their livestock to Penistone market.

We now head down the track along Mickleden Edge to Langsett village and its reservoir. We will soon be back to the landscape of green fields and woodlands, back to civilisation, away from the wild open moors. But we can look back, physically and mentally, to our great achievement: a day to remember, a place of tranquillity and solitude, not a place for the faint-hearted; a stiff climb and difficult terrain, its rewards all the better for the effort - an Everest climbed.

ROUTE 8 - The Ramble that SCAM Never Did

by Terry Howard

We never got round to doing this former trespass walk as a group, but several individual SCAM members walked it frequently. It is a walk of much interest, offering opportunities to rediscover lost features of the landscape.

The walk follows the Yorkshire and Derbyshire boundary from Moscar via Strines Edge onto Dovestone Tor on Derwent Edge. I recall researching this walk and enquiring about the legality of following the line of the boundary. It must have been legal in the past because people kept the custom of beating the bounds of their parish every Rogation Sunday. This county boundary is also part of the parish boundary of Hathersage in Derbyshire and Bradfield in Yorkshire, as well as part of the township boundary of Derwent. Further back in time, the boundary would have marked part of the larger parish boundaries of Hope in Derbyshire and Ecclesfield in Yorkshire.

My endeavours to find a legal way of following the boundary over Strines Edge to Dovestone Tor didn't lead to a definite answer, but as the boundary also delineated two properties, it was deemed not to have public right of way status at that point. This in itself should have generated interest in making it a SCAM trespass ramble. It didn't, but it can now be considered a legal route, thanks to the 2000 CROW Act.

Start at the county boundary at Moscar and go up Heathy Lane, passing Moscar Lodge on the left. This lodge was built for Mark Firth, a Sheffield industrialist and owner of moorland in this area. Just past the lodge is a gate which gives the only easy access onto Parson's Piece. This parcel of land was given to the vicar of Hathersage under the 1830 Hathersage Enclosure Award in lieu of tithes, and the vicar eventually sold it on.

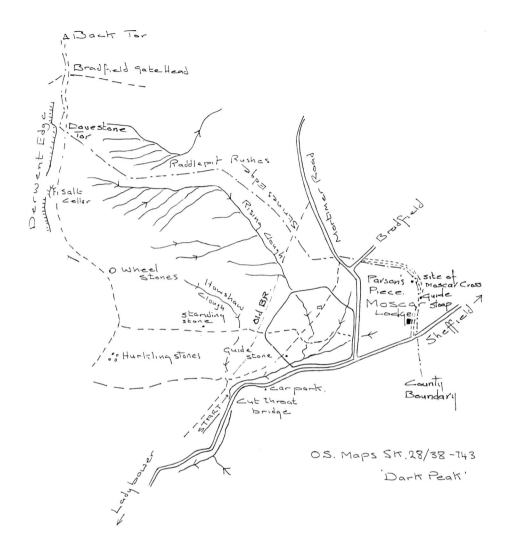

A Back Tor

Bradfield gate Head

Derwent Edge

Dovestone Tor

Paddlepit Rushes

Sirening Clough

Rising Clough

Moscar Road

Bradfield

salt cellar

o Wheel Stones

Howshaw Clough

Parson's Piece.

site of Moscar Cross

guide stoop

Moscar Lodge.

standing stone

old BR

Sheffield

Hurkling stones

Guide stone

County Boundary

car park.

Cut throat bridge

START

Ladybower

O.S. Maps SK.28/38 -743

'Dark Peak'

The wall to the right as you go up Heathy Lane follows the boundary, so you are walking in Derbyshire. At the junction with Stake Hill Road on the right, and where there is a large guide stone on the left of Heathy Lane, the walk passes into Yorkshire. From here, the left-hand wall up, over and down Moscar Cross Road to Sugworth Road is the boundary, so the walk is continuing in Yorkshire. The guide stone is often confused with Moscar Cross (or Humble Stone Cross). Moscar Cross itself is around the slight bend in the wall as you go up Moscar Cross Road. It served as a parish and county boundary marker and was probably one of many such crosses on a processional route between parish churches. It was vandalised sometime after the Hathersage Enclosure Award but was shown in place on contemporary maps. The only remnant of the cross is part of the mortice base near one of the holloways in Parson's Piece.

Cross Sugworth Road from Moscar Cross Road. The boundary continues diagonally from Sugworth Road to Strines Lane, following the line of the wall - some stone boundary markers can be found at either end of this short section of wall. Here you briefly leave the boundary to enable safe access onto the moor via the gate on the left. Cross the heather back to the boundary, which is marked by small standing stones. A vehicle track runs adjacent to the boundary along Strines Edge. However, to see the many stone boundary markers you must keep walking off this vehicle track. The stones are inscribed with various marks, including 'H' for Hathersage and 'D' for Derwent, the latter referring to the reservoir-submerged village.

A short distance along Strines Edge a holloway ascends from Rising Clough and then descends towards the Mortimer Road, or Strines Lane as it is called at this point. This holloway was the old bridleway, shown on Jeffrey's map of 1772, leading from Hope to Penistone, approximately on the same route as the later Mortimer Road, built in 1777, but respecting the contours more, even though that made it more circuitous. It was probably a packhorse route along which wares from Derbyshire and Yorkshire were transported.

On Strines Moor the boundary leads west, then north west, to Dovestone Tor. The vehicle track heads west to Raddlepit Rushes, 'rushes' warning that the way ahead is very wet at times, and 'raddlepit' referring to a pit from which the red ochre, raddle or reddle, was extracted for use in marking sheep. When the vehicle track disappears you are left to find the boundary markers. This section is not easy and can be challenging. I always find it more convenient at this point to use compass bearings set on Dovestone Tor and follow areas of short or burned heather while keeping to the general bearing.

On arrival at Dovestone Tor the options for your return are many: south by paths to Ladybower; north and then west by paths to Fairholmes, north then east by paths to Bradfield; or south then east by paths back to Moscar. My preference is west to John Field Howden, around Far and Near Deep Cloughs towards Hollins Clough and the new access points in that area, down to the side of Derwent Reservoir and then on to Fairholmes.

Boundary marker stone on Strines Edge. (Terry Howard)

THE RIGHT TO ROAM

by Terry Howard

A speech given to the Local Access Forum on November 8, 2003

The campaign for access to open country - mountain and moorland - has a long history. Its roots may stretch back to when people were dispossessed of the land they held and worked, or upon which they exercised common rights. We hear of Norman barons taking land from previous owners, peasants' revolts, emparkment of villages and field, land clearances and enclosures. In Sheffield, at Crookesmoor, the militia were called out to quell a riot over the loss of common rights on that moor. People have always had an attachment to, or relationship with, the land which they believed they had a moral right to use.

The Countryside and Rights of Way Act (2000) grew in part from these roots, as well as from the campaigns and trespasses of the late nineteenth and early twentieth centuries, and the more recent campaigns of groups like Sheffield Campaign for Access to Moorland. These later campaigns though were not so much concerned with land ownership as with gaining access to mountain and moorland for recreational purposes, particularly fresh air and exercise.

After the First World War more and more people wanted to escape, if only briefly, from squalid living and working conditions to the fresher air and beauty of the countryside. However these weekend migrations were strictly limited in terms of routes and destinations. Even popular locations now taken for granted - Stanage, Froggatt Edge, Mam Tor, Kinder Scout and Win Hill - were all out of bounds, except to those who were prepared to exercise what they believed to be their ancient rights by trespassing. Continued frustration led to events which have now become part of our social history.

Two such events were the Kinder Trespass of April 1932, after which six ramblers were imprisoned, and the September 1932 Abbey Brook Trespass, which was both a response to the imprisonments and an attempt to regain an ancient path across moorland. Both these events made a major contribution to the campaign for access to moorland, swelling the attendances at mass rallies annually held in the Winnats Pass and later Cave Dale at Castleton. Most of the support came from ramblers who lived in the Manchester and Sheffield areas. The hoped-for access did not materialise but the campaigns did generate much wider interest and concern throughout the country, and they paved the way for future more successful access campaigns.

The breakthrough seemed to come after the Second World War, with the 1949 National Parks and Access to Countryside Act. The Act promised greater access to mountain and moorland through Access Agreements with landowners, but although the Peak District saw several gains in access, most open country remained closed to ramblers.

In 1982 at Bowden Bridge quarry near Hayfield, a rally was held to mark the 50th anniversary of the 1932 Kinder Scout Mass Trespass, and it was addressed by Benny Rothman, one of the imprisoned leaders in 1932. Benny, who had served six months imprisonment for 'riotous assembly', helped to kick-start the access movement which seemed to have run out of steam in the post-war years.

In Sheffield a group had organised support for the 50th anniversary celebrations in Hayfield, even having a mass trespass on Bamford Moor before the Hayfield rally, and in May 1982 the group called itself Sheffield Campaign for Access to Moorland, or SCAM. SCAM now took the initiative and organised further trespasses, and these awakened within the Ramblers' Association the need to campaign again for the access to mountains and moorland which the 1949 Act had promised but generally failed to deliver. The RA took up the challenge, and through its organising and campaigning we now have the Countryside and Rights of Way Act, 2000.

SCAM - 'POLITICS' AND 'pOLITICS'

by Terry Howard

SCAM's policy was that of campaigning for a legal right for everyone to have access on foot to moorland. In that sense SCAM was 'political', but not in a 'party political' sense: SCAM never wanted to be 'party political' even though many SCAM members did have a 'party political' leaning.

In its early days SCAM attracted a few animal rights activists and the occasional anarchist, but these people didn't stay long, as they soon realised that SCAM was only about campaigning for public access to moorland. Although this was considered a leftish ideal, many SCAM supporters were more broad church in their political leanings.

I was a youth leader in the Woodcraft Folk, whose history from the 1920s included the principles of co-operation, internationalism and support for human rights (including children's rights), and whose activities included anti-fascist and anti-war rallies as well as the campaign for the right to roam over all the country's mountains and moorland.

My initial involvement with SCAM was as a representative of the Woodcraft Folk. The latter was a uniformed organisation, and as such we were not allowed by law or the Charities Act to support 'party political' activities. Like the peace demonstrations in the 1980s, the campaign for access to moorland was considered to be non-party political and so the Woodcraft Folk could join in, wearing our green shirts.

The first SCAM trespass ramble, which took place on Bamford Moor, was very well-attended and it included many green-shirted Woodcraft Folk, proud to be continuing the tradition of access campaigning of the 1930s and 1940s. We attended the 50th Anniversary of the 1932 Kinder Trespass, walking over from Edale to Bowden Bridge in Hayfield, and there were many Woodcrafters, some from as far away as London. As we walked down towards the gathering throng at Bowden Bridge, we were elated to be part of this new awakening and to be reflecting the aspirations of the young people of Britain. Benny Rothman was an inspiration as he addressed us, just as he addressed a similar crowd 50 years previously. Although he died in 2002 just before the enactment of the CROW Act, he remains an inspiration.

I was fully aware of the early access campaigns, having been weaned on such stories as that of the Abbey Brook Trespass of 1932. The Hayfield rally in 1982 cemented my commitment to the cause of public access to moorlands, and SCAM became the vehicle that carried my commitment.

View from the head of William Clough, Kinder, on the 50th anniversary walk of the Kinder Trespass in 1982. (Peak District National Park)

I was a regular attender and contributor to SCAM's activities, whether meetings or trespass walks, and I made sure that the aspirations of young people were placed on the agenda. Although initially the emphasis was on raising the profile of access by trespassing, SCAM started to take on board other related issues. These included responding to the threat of loss of access on newly-privatised Water Authority land; consultations on the Peak National Park Plan and the Upper Don Tributary Study, both of which promised increased access to moorland; and management proposals for moorland newly-acquired by the Peak Park Planning Board - Big Moor, Ramsley Moor, Leash Fen and the Roaches. SCAM also produced a leaflet called *The Enclosure Acts: How We Lost the Moors*, written by Jim Byford.

One of the meetings hosted by the Peak Park was the annual Footpath and Access meeting held at Buxton. The participants were the Peak Park Joint Planning Board members, their officers and various user groups, mostly from walking organisations. Over the years SCAM was continually refused representation, not by the PPJPB itself but by a consensus of the other walking groups. Because SCAM was refused entry, a demonstration took place outside the Old Hall Hotel where the meeting was taking place.

However when I started attending on behalf of the Ramblers' Association the situation changed. Everyone in attendance knew I was a SCAM member, indeed SCAM Secretary, even though I was there to represent the Ramblers' Association. They even knew I was furthering the cause of SCAM and that SCAM was effectively being represented by my presence. It wasn't long before SCAM's philosophy on access became the consensus.

To promote and publicise the continuing access campaign, SCAM produced a tape/slide show, *Trespassers Will Be Celebrated*, and a booklet, *Freedom of the Moors*. The tape/slide show was produced by Alan Pond, a fresh convert to the access campaign who wanted to record where it had come from, where it stood now and where it seemed to be going. Over many years the show was well used and well received, being seen by many organisations, from local rambling groups to an Agricultural College. Although some of its contents may now seem questionable in terms of accuracy, it reflected current thinking at the time. In particular the recording of voices of past campaigners, many now sadly deceased, make it second to none as a historical record.

More controversial was *Freedom of the Moors*, the booklet of trespass walks in the Peak District National Park. Although other books had been published about access, this was the only one actively and positively urging trespass. Though the booklet was launched at Sheffield Town Hall, we were told that one councillor had attempted to get the proceedings stopped, as she said it encouraged people to break the law. Nothing happened though, and the booklet was sold in many shops, including the

Council's foyer shop in the Central Library. In the Peak District National Park things were different – although the booklet was available in some shops, the Peak Park Joint Planning Board refused to sell it in any of its Information Centres. Despite all this the booklet was a great success.

At the Festival of National Parks held at Chatsworth in September, 1987, the culmination of a three-year National Parks Awareness Campaign, SCAM joined with the Ramblers' Association and Sheffield City Council to produce a leaflet for distribution at the event. At the time there was no general public access to the Chatsworth Estate moorlands. The event was high profile and included Diana, Princess of Wales as guest of honour. SCAM lobbied the entrance to Chatsworth and handed out the leaflet, which was entitled *Watch over, but don't walk through, our National Parks*. We were not prevented from handing out the leaflet, though the security guards kept their eyes on us.

Perhaps one of SCAM's greatest achievements was to get Sheffield City Council to include in its policies total support for access to open country, mountain, moorland and mature woodland. This was achieved through our involvement with the Countryside Working Party and the production of the policy document, *Out and About* in Sheffield's Countryside. SCAM has continued to enjoy the support of Sheffield City Council, and across all the political parties. Several Lord Mayors' Civic Receptions have been held for SCAM activists.

SCAM is unique in the sense that no other organisation has had a continuing programme of regular trespass walks. Although the earlier walks were intended to raise public awareness of the lack of access, later walks developed into enabling the public to be aware of what they were missing by not being allowed onto the moors. In taking on this educational role, we gained acknowledgement as an organisation not only firm in its resolve to gain public access to moorland, but as a responsible body.

It is interesting to note that on the early walks we always found locked gates left unlocked and keepers conspicuous by their absence. It is believed that landowners saw to this, perhaps after police advice as a tactic to avoid confrontations. Maybe landowners had the impression that if nothing happened and there was no trouble, SCAM would just have its walk and then eventually disappear into the sunset.

Although there was minimal response to our walks from most landowners, we wanted them and the Peak Park Joint Planning Board (now the Peak District National Park Authority) to know we were still out there trespassing. Whenever a trespass was organised we always signalled our intentions to the landowners or their agents. Occasionally we invited them to join us, but they never took us up! Similarly the police were always informed of our plans. In effect many of the trespass rambles became quite polite affairs, but the walks were logged and landowners were left in no doubt that SCAM would continue until access was gained.

We were always concerned that we should not be labelled as criminal or irresponsible activists. We avoided any sort of damage to property, and far from leaving litter we often picked up the litter left by others, including shooting syndicates, gamekeepers and farmers, who tended to be the only other people on non-access land. We also had a policy of not taking dogs on our walks because we thought it might undermine or detract from the campaign for access. Some SCAM supporters had a problem with this policy, but we knew landowners were particularly concerned about dogs on moorland, and the 2000 CROW Act has had to take this into account.

Looking back over SCAM's history, we were radical in reviving and continuing past campaigns, but we were also responsible, showing that we could work with landowners, given the opportunity. At our AGM in 1992, for instance, our guest speaker was John Lees of the Moorland Owners and Tenants Association, and we found we had a lot of common ground. I even invited him to join SCAM, but he said he didn't think his clients would approve! The pursuit of access was never for its own sake or to follow some party political dogma. It was a means to open up our moorland heritage for the enjoyment, education and creativity of everyone.

On September 19, 2004 we could at last legally set foot on formerly forbidden moorlands, and the implementation of the 2000 CROW Act was launched at rallies held in the Peak District and the Forest of Bowland. There was an atmosphere of thankfulness rather than euphoria at getting to this landmark; thankfulness that the campaign was won and we could now get on with enjoying what we had waited for over many years. At first it all seemed like a dream - access signs in place, new stiles and gates being erected, new access maps for the Peak District.

On September 29, 2004 the Lord Mayor of Sheffield, Councillor Mike Pye, a SCAM member and active access supporter, held a civic reception at Sheffield Town Hall for SCAM activists and other access supporters, plus councillors from all three of the main political parties, all of who were unanimous in congratulating and thanking SCAM for all its access work. On October 6, 2004 a motion was put to a full Sheffield City Council meeting by Councillor Peter Price, congratulating and thanking all access campaigners in Sheffield.

Terry Howard presents the SCAM plaque to Sheffield's Lord Mayor, Pat Midgeley, at Sheffield Town Hall. (Terry Howard)

It was passed unanimously. At the Ramblers' Association General Council in Nottingham, a motion was passed thanking SCAM and all past and present access campaigners for helping to bring about the 2000 CROW Act. It too was passed unanimously.

So what is the future of SCAM? Now we have the 2000 CROW Act, is SCAM's work finished? Decidedly no – there is still a lot to be done. We have to make sure access is established by encouraging people to use the newly-opened moorlands. We can help to educate people to use the moors responsibly and to enjoy their benefits. We can continue to campaign to make sure the 2000 CROW Act is fully implemented, with access being extended to mature woodlands and riverbanks. We can campaign to make the 2000 CROW Act at least as good in its implications for access as the Scottish and Scandinavian models. We can continue to participate in Local Access Forums or any other bodies which have access on their agendas.

Perhaps one of the most poignant things to me is that SCAM followed in the footsteps of past campaigners. When I first put my feet legally onto Bamford Moor – site of SCAM's first trespass – I couldn't help thinking of all those generations of access comrades we had lost on the way, who could never share with us the fruits of their endeavours. We owe them a debt of gratitude and must always remember them – Bert Ward, Edwin Royce, Phil Daley, Steve Morton, Benny Rothman, Howard Hill, Bill Keen, Shirley Meek, George Fowler, Walt Grocock, Archie Brearley and many many more. It is incumbent upon us to protect our new freedom – the freedom to roam on open country.

CROW IMPLEMENTED

by Les Seaman

Sunday, September 19, 2004 was a historic date for all users of the countryside. From that date a major new right of access was gradually introduced, giving people the opportunity to walk freely across mapped access land without having to stay on footpaths.

The areas opened up under CROW 2000 are shown on the new Ordnance Survey maps. Access onto these moors, according to the Act, can be from any adjacent road or right of way, over a stile or through an access gate or field gate, and it is envisaged that new access points will be put in at convenient points close to roads and rights of way.

To help ramblers access these moorlands, a list of new and existing access points is being compiled by the Ramblers' Association for the area west and north of Sheffield. Unfortunately the OS maps will not be showing access points, only the area of access land, so this information will only be available through the Ramblers' Association.

These new rights cover most recreational activities carried out on foot, including walking, sightseeing, birdwatching, climbing and running. Dogs are generally welcome to accompany their owners, but owners should be aware of when they have to keep their animals on leads and when specific exclusions are applied to dogs. The new right requires you to keep your dog on a lead of no more than two metres long between March 1 and July 31(the main breeding season for ground-nesting birds) or any time of the year when you are near livestock. Specific local restrictions may also be in place – for instance dogs are excluded from the new access lands to the west of Sheffield, and signs indicating this will be displayed.

Farmers and landowners have the discretion to suspend or restrict the new access right for 28 days each year, for any reason, except Bank Holidays, no more than four Saturdays/Sundays a year, no Saturdays between June 1 and August 11 and no Sundays between June 1 and September 30. They may also apply for long-term restrictions or closures where necessary for land management, safety or fire prevention reasons. Whenever possible, restrictions and closures can be checked by ringing 0845 100 3298, and will be reinforced by signs on the ground. A policy of least restrictive practice will be adopted within the Peak District National Park so that closures will be limited in duration and area in order that we can access the moors with as little inconvenience as possible.

An old-style 'Boundary of Open Country' sign on the Eastern Moors. (Peak District National Park)

THE MAGIC OF THE MOORS

by Terry Howard

The moors are our wilderness, but they are not an untouched, primeval wilderness. They have been influenced and changed by human presence for thousands of years. Daniel Defoe famously referred to the Derbyshire moors as 'the most desolate, wild, and abandoned country in all England' and a 'howling wilderness'. Adventurous and enquiring walkers, perhaps influenced by Wordsworth and others, have thought differently.

Both the popular Stanage Edge and the large expanse of Broomhead Moor offer a wilderness experience. Whether the wilderness is actual or just perceived, the effect is the same - trudging through peat bogs, scrambling over groughs, discovering a hidden valley and waterfall, stumbling across the ruins of a forgotten age, fighting a way through a raging blizzard, being lashed by driving rain, seeing and smelling the purple heather, dipping hot and tired feet into a cool mountain stream, or drinking the pure, cold water from a mountain spring.

Our moorland now is only a remnant of what it was just a few hundred years ago. Many of Sheffield's moors - like Ranmoor and Crookesmoor - have been built over for many generations. Hawksworth Firth was a vast moorland area covering much of the parish of Bradfield, but it has been reduced by the advance of agricultural settlement and the later Parliamentary Enclosure of 1826. The place name is no longer in use, and the largest remnants are the Bradfield Moors of Strines and Thornseat.

Even these could have been lost to agriculture after being divided up and allotted to various 'common rights' owners in 1826. The Enclosure Award stated that these allotments were to be fenced or walled by their owners. It is arguable that these moors survive because the allotments were purchased by a single owner whose interest was not agriculture but 'sport'. Grouse shooting, then in its infancy, required large open areas of heather moorland, as a result of which no fences or walls were erected.

Grouse moor management involves the creation of a heather monoculture in which heather is rotationally cut or burned in strips, usually in a 12-year cycle. Fresh young shoots of heather from these strips provide the grouses' staple diet, while old, long, and leggy heather provides cover for breeding. The moors look spectacular in August, carpeted with purple heather, but from above or from a distance they can look like a chequered quilt, or figures from the Nazco Desert of Peru.

From a walker's point of view, the burning and cutting of heather makes it easier to cross the large expanses of moorland, with less waist-high heather to struggle through. Another great facilitator is the presence of sheep tracks, which meander across the moors and are easy to follow, though in both cases the walker will tend to be walking in long zigzags rather than short straight lines. Another by-product of burning and cutting regimes is the occasional exposure of lost settlements, building foundations, burial mounds and stone circles. All this makes the moors fascinating and mysterious places.

The wildlife on the moors complements this fascination - curlews piping through the mist, golden plovers wheeling across the walker's path, ravens croaking from the tors, raptors of various kinds circling high above - all these add to the thrill. Lately, deer have started to colonise one area, and to come across them creates a dilemma - whether to press on and thereby scatter them or whether to retreat and leave them in peace. White or mountain hares, which from a distance look like remnants of winter snow, soon come to life and dart away. Most walkers will have their own tales to tell of encounters with wildlife on the moors. My most impressive experience was seeing an osprey climbing in ever increasing circles above Howden moors.

Each moorland area is different in terms of wildlife and cultural heritage, and this rests on geology and geomorphology. The Dark Peak moors are made up of gritstone, sandstone and shales, the gritstone often outlining the edges of the dip and scarp slopes of the land, with Kinder and Bleaklow rising above. Sandstone often marks lesser edges, with shales in between.

On these edges and higher up we find much evidence of human activity, transitory or more permanent. Settlements often face roughly towards the south west to take full advantage of the sun. Neolithic and Bronze Age people left their mark on the landscapes and I believe it is no coincidence that their sites overlook the Derwent valley or look towards Kinder Scout, on which very few burial sites have yet been found. Were the Derwent and Kinder regarded as sacred? Was Kinder seen as a resting place for the spirits of the dead?

All the moors offer a variety of experiences. They can offer a challenge to walkers - the physical challenge and an opportunity to practice navigational skills. They can offer the educational experience of discovering the moorland heritage - the geology, wildlife, evidence of human occupation, management and conservation. They can offer the spiritual experience of retreating for a short time from city life for the purposes of reflection and recharging. And they can offer possibilities for inspiration which can be expressed in drawing, painting, writing, photography and so on.

The moors are alive and, like us, they have their moods - they can seduce, threaten, pacify, challenge, befriend or even alienate. People have co-existed with these moors for thousands of years, and this co-existence relies on understanding them and using them responsibly. Through this respect we can ensure that future generations will continue to discover and enjoy the relationship.

Overleaf: The magic of the moors: Kinder Reservoir from William Clough.
(Peak District National Park)